FIRST NATIONAL EDITION

PRACTICAL
DIVORCE
SOLUTIONS

BY ED SHERMAN
DIVORCE SPECIALIST ATTORNEY

Nolo Press
Occidental

P O Box 7 2 2
Occidental CA 95465
(7 0 7) 8 7 4 - 3 1 0 5

Design and Graphics: Charles Ed Sherman
Drawing, page 30: Angel Strehlen

Sources—these books were invaluable resources:
The Divorce Book, by McKay, Rogers, Blades & Gosse. New Harbinger
Publications. An excellent popular guidebook.
Mediate Your Divorce, by Joan Blades, Prentice Hall.
The Process of Divorce: How Professionals and Couples Negotiate Divorce, by Kenneth Kressel, Basic Books. This very readable academic study
gathers together everything known about divorce settlements in the literature of social science.

First California Edition: May, 1988
Second California Edition: August, 1990
First National Edition: January, 1994

ISBN 0-944508-13-8
Library of Congress No. 88-060307

CONTENTS

After a while you learn the subtle difference between
    holding a hand and chaining a soul,

And you learn that love doesn't mean leaning
    and company doesn't mean security,

And you begin to learn that kisses aren't contracts
    and presents aren't promises,

And you begin to accept your defeats with your head
    up and your eyes open, with the grace of an adult,
    not the grief of a child,

And you learn to live your life today because
    tomorrow's ground is too uncertain for plans.

After a while you learn that even sunshine burns
    if you get too much.

So plant your own garden and decorate your own soul
    instead of waiting for someone to bring you flowers.

And you learn that you really can endure....that you really
    are strong,

And you really do have worth.

                                        —Anonymous

This book is dedicated, with love, to my ex-wife
from whom I learned so very much
about the subjects in these pages.

Acknowledgements

Special mention—

Trudy Ahlstrom, who keeps the Nolo Press operation going in Occidental. She's good—I mean, folks, she's re-e-e-eally good, as were her invaluable contributions to this book.
Lynda Barrad, who gave so much warm support, good ideas and jovial encouragement.

Contributors—

I'm in awe at the number of people who have helped get the book (and me) this far, and grateful to have had the help of such outstanding people. Without them, it would have been a longer, harder job with much less to show at the end. It is impossible to rank them, so they appear in alphabetical order.

Thanks to:

• **Marje Burdine**, Director (and founder) of the Conflict Resolution Department at the Justice Institute, an arm of the Attorney General of British Columbia—for an exhaustive critique.
• **Rosemary Carter**, of Carter Communications, Vancouver, BC; a brilliant wordsmith and all-around good person to know (Bill too)—for keen editing.
• **Joel Edelman**, attorney, mediator, teacher—for insights into mediation.
• **Michael Fogel**, attorney, ex-judge from Los Angeles, metamorphosed into a new career in conflict resolution in Vancouver—for a valuable critique.
• **Betty Goldwater**, family counselor, Santa Barbara, a dear friend with deep insights and a great, generous heart.

• **Art Gottlieb**, attorney, playwrite—nepotism at its best.
• **Heather Hutchinson** and **Will Malloff**, dear friends in attendance at many a midnight debriefing.
• **Marty & Susan Hykin**, cherished friends, world-class minds—for fine feedback.
• **Jim Johnson**, Ph.D., Dean of Psychology turned entrepreneur and designer of applied psychology software—for incisive criticism.
• **Hugh McIsaac**, President, American Assoc. of Family and Conciliation Courts, an international society; Director of Los Angeles County Family Court Services; and a damn fine man —for information and insights into California's mandatory mediation and divorce generally.

• **Tasha Schaal**, founder of Divorce Anonymous, a national support organization based in Los Angeles—for networking and moral support.
• **Lee Tuley**, Rennaisance woman, brilliant keeper of the crystal heart—gives good feedback, and great ideas, too.
• **Publishers Group West**, Charlie and the whole gang, for their consistent support and good ideas over the years.
• **Peggy Williams & Anne Lober**, Attorneys and mediators, now partners in the Divorce Helpline, for their valuable critique, fresh ideas and priceless friendship.
Teri Woods, film-maker, songwriter, leprechuan, druid and, above all else, a bearer of the light.

"In a time of turbulence and change
. . . knowledge is power."

—John F. Kennedy (1962)
paraphrasing Francis Bacon (1597).

1

How to Get the Best Possible Divorce

The question now is not *if* you will get a divorce—the question is what *kind* of divorce will you have to go through? What price will you have to pay to get through it? How hard will it have to be on you—and the children, if you have any?

Isn't there some *good* way to get through it easier and cheaper?

YES!

We definitely *do* know how you can make your divorce better. You know, of course, that no one can just wave a wand and make all your troubles go away. Divorce is never pleasant. But the right information can put you in control and make your divorce smoother, faster, cheaper, less aggravating and less painful than it otherwise might be.

This book is based on over 25 years of experience. About 4,000 people a year use our Divorce Helpline service in California and over 600,000 couples have used our *How To Do Your Own Divorce* books in California and Texas. We also include the best information and ideas from dozens of professional studies. This information is tried and tested. It has helped others and it will help you.

This year, over 160,000 California couples will start the divorce journey. About 95,000 in Texas, maybe 80,000 in Florida—all together, nearly 1.5 million couples across the U.S. will start a divorce this year. So what? Who cares about all those other people? When there's a rock on your foot, you tend to lose interest in the view from the mountain. Yet, the fact is that you can benefit greatly from the experience of those millions who have gone before you. You can learn the best routes and how to avoid common traps and pitfalls. You can save yourself a lot of time, trouble, and money.

Start with the right information. Usually, people start into a divorce without bothering to find out anything about the rules, where they are going or how to get there. This is understandable, considering the upset of divorce, *but it is a very dangerous and costly mistake!* A survey of people who have used our divorce books shows that perhaps the single most important factor in having a better divorce is starting off with the right information, and having the control over your life that gives you.

So congratulate yourself. The fact that you are reading this book shows you have a desire to know and to participate that will lead you to successful solutions. That strength of character is one of your great assets—you are already on a good path.

The worst path and an alternative

The worst thing a person can possibly do is go off to some lawyer without any information or preparation and just ask for a divorce.

Want to know what happens when you go into a lawyer's office and you don't know anything? Well, first of all, how do you know you've got a good lawyer? And even if the lawyer is good, how do you know you've got the right *kind* of good lawyer? It would be an advantage to know how to pick your lawyer, wouldn't it?

Then, how do you know what to ask for? If you don't know what you can get from the law, you might be expecting a kind of help that you can't get —or you might expect too much from the kind of help that you *can* get. Or you might not be expecting enough. If your expectations are off, you can end up frustrated and angry at your lawyer for the wrong reasons.

Next, the lawyer obviously has to find out about your case, so you sit there at $150 an hour telling practically your whole life's story because you want to get it off your chest and because you don't know what's really relevant to the legal issues—in fact, you have no idea what the legal issues are—and the lawyer has to sort it all out and untangle your story like a ball of snarled twine. Or, maybe be inhibited by uncertainty and clam up, leaving the lawyer to dig your story out of you bit by bit—at about $150 an hour.

Then you need to ask a lot of questions so you can find out what's going to happen and you probably have to go home to dig up some more information and maybe get some documents, then you have to take it all back for another office visit and ask more questions. This all takes a lot of time—at about $150 an hour.

And how do you feel? Ignorant and helpless.

Divorce tends to be undermining anyway, so it would be absolutely normal for you to feel insecure, inadequate, not in control of your own life. That's *before* you go uninformed and unprepared into some lawyer's office and reinforce those unpleasant feelings. It gets worse when you find out, as so often happens, that your lawyer is hard to reach and doesn't bother to help you understand what's going on in your case.

Now look what would happen if you knew what you were doing ahead of time—that is, if you had good information and were well prepared.

First of all, you might not have to go to a lawyer at all. If you *did* want a lawyer, you might be able to see one just for specific advice or for a limited service. In *any* case, you would know how to choose and how to use the right lawyer.

When you went in you would have your information and documents prepared ahead of time so you would just hand it all over and not waste much time on the facts. You would tell the lawyer exactly what you wanted to know and what you wanted to accomplish, and you would *not* have to ask so many dumb questions and feel helpless.

So you have already saved hundreds, maybe thousands of dollars, haven't you?

And what effect do you think this has on your lawyer? Well, the lawyer is very aware of dealing with a client who knows what's what—and you'd better believe *that* makes a big difference. You're going to get a whole different kind of treatment—better care and more respect!

And how does this feel to you, personally? Absolutely great! You are *not* helpless, you are *not* the victim of external forces. You *do* know what's going on, you *are* in control of your own life and you are doing a good job under difficult circumstances.

And what do you get? More respect! This time, your own.

Uncontrolled battle. The worse result of going uninformed and unprepared to a lawyer is that you are likely to end up in some sort of uncontrolled battle where the lawyer is in charge of your divorce—your life—and you are not. Contrary to what you might expect, being represented by a lawyer feels awful.

Even simple, unopposed cases cost a lot, but what's worse is that your case is likely to get stirred up into increased conflict and even higher cost. Fees of $2,000 to $10,000 for *each* spouse are considered cheap for *simple* cases in big cities, while $7,000 to $20,000 each is ordinary, and it can easily run well over $50,000 *each* if the case has conflict. In big money cases, a $200,000 fee on each side is no surprise. Of course, few lawyers start off quoting such figures; you are more likely to hear their hourly rate and an optimistic estimate. Fees aside, uncontrolled battles tend to drag on and on for a very long time, wearing you down, burdening your life.

You may driven to call a lawyer by your own insecurity and fears—you just don't think you can cope, you don't know the rules or how to deal with your spouse. Or maybe it's red-hot anger that sends you to a lawyer, like pushing the ultimate button. You might show your spouse a thing or two, but you might also trap yourself on the blind path to an uncontrolled divorce. Either way, you show up there in a rush, uninformed and unprepared. This is what we want you to avoid.

The more emotionally distressed you are about your divorce, the more attractive it might seem just to turn the whole ugly mess over to a lawyer—but doing so almost never works out to your advantage. In the first place, lawyers don't handle the whole divorce, just the strictly legal aspects. Very few of your real–life problems will be addressed, but no one points this out, so you may have unreasonable expectations of what your lawyer can do for you. Then you suffer the frustration of finding out, eventually, that your problems have not been handed over after all—they've followed you home. They are still all yours, and you may have sprouted a whole new set of legal and financial problems as well.

Uncontrolled battle arouses the worst instincts in all parties. It will be very hard on you. If there are children, an uncontrolled battle is terrible because children are always victims of the emotional and legal warfare between their parents.

If you don't know what's going on and if you can't control the legal game to your own advantage, you will face the financial trauma of uncontrolled legal expense. You will end up completely in the dark, an ignorant bystander in your own life. You will feel helpless ....and you may be right.

The alternative to the worst path: The only way to protect yourself and get the kind of results you want is to be fully informed and prepared *before* you begin, to be in charge of your own case as much as possible—which is what this book is all about.

Three keys to a better divorce

Be informed and be prepared. The only way you can avoid the blind path that leads to an uncontrolled divorce is by becoming informed and prepared. It isn't hard and the results are worth it. People who know what's going on invariably get better divorces than those who do not.

Control your case. A Connecticut study (1976) showed that of couples with lawyers, about 60% worked out *all* their own terms without resort to their attorneys, meaning that in most cases the clients do most of the real work anyway. More important is a study in New Jersey (1984) showing that *client control of divorce negotiations is the most significant predictor of a good post-divorce outcome.* "Good outcome" includes things like better compliance with agreements, less chance of litigation, increased good-will, better co-parenting. This means that whether or not you use a lawyer, if you control your own case you will save money, reduce aggravation, and feel good about being in charge of your own life.

Taking control does not mean you can't get help or seek advice, it means that you take responsibility for knowing what's going on and for making your own decisions. You become an active participant in the negotiations. You take responsibility for your own actions and feelings. That's healthy and that's what works.

Keep business and personal matters separate. Many aspects of getting through a divorce are business-like in nature: money, property, procedures, negotiation and agreements, lawyers and taxes. Business and personal/ emotional matters do *not* mix well. The best way to protect yourself, to reduce conflict and confusion, is to keep business matters as separate as possible from emotional and personal concerns. This does not mean that you don't deal with personal and emotional matters—just not at the same time you are taking care of business.

2

The Divorce Roadmap
and an overview

You can think of your divorce as having to go on a difficult journey across unknown, rugged territory—something like the early settlers faced when they had to get across the real Great Divide, the terrifying Rocky Mountains.

Behind you is a life you can no longer live. Before you is a future with more hope and possibilities, but first you have to get across some forboding terrain with traps, dangers and pitfalls. You stand there with your life's accumulations, fighting fear, trying to find the means and the courage to go into the unknown ....when suddenly someone shows up with a map and a book of information about the journey.

It may not be an easy trip, but you certainly do not have to go cross-country with no map or compass. Others have already marked all the best ways for you, and if you take a popular route there will be way-stations, traveler's aid services and even fellow travelers. What you need to do now is study the maps and the latest travel information before you start. You don't want to just wander off into your divorce, you want to go prepared.

So, like any good traveller encountering unknown terrain, you climb a tree to get an overview of the territory you have to cross. Okay, then—here's your map and a view from a tree.

Map notes

Study the map for a bit and try to get a sense of the possible paths you can take. The notes below are a brief summary of what each part of the map is about.

THE REAL DIVORCE: The legal divorce is a ceremony you have to go through to legally dissolve the bonds of matrimony, but your "real" divorce is about you and your life as you live it. The real divorce is about ending one life and beginning another; it's what you go

THE DIVORCE ROADMAP

THE REAL DIVORCE
emotional, spiritual
& practical matters

Your spouse won't oppose you because gone or doesn't care

GET INFORMATION
Learn about divorce

Both spouses are involved and care...

...possibly in active disagreement

WORK ON AGREEMENT
Negotiation • Mediation
Self help • Counseling

START THE LEGAL DIVORCE

Go to lawyer without learning about divorce

Get a *good* lawyer
who is trained in mediation.
Start legal action and negotiation.

Lawyer takes over

Loss of Control

Breakdown of communications

through in practical, emotional and spiritual terms—and these matters are only incidentally addressed by the legal divorce. The real divorce is about breaking old patterns, finding a new center for your life, doing your best with the hand you've been dealt.

Your ability to solve your practical problems will be greatly improved if you understand some basic things about the emotional stages you and your spouse might go through. Also, there are many traps in the emotional jungle that you can avoid if you are aware of

WHY TRAVEL WITHOUT A MAP

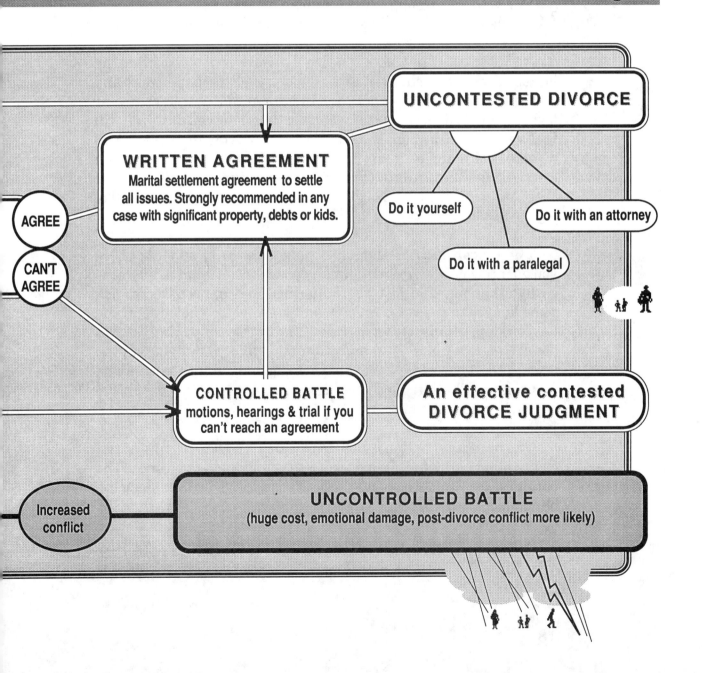

them. If you want to deal with emotional issues, there are some good techniques you can try and many support groups you can turn to for help. For example, you can use the system of "structured problem-solving" to help you get through your practical, emotional and legal problems. All this is what Chapter 3 is about.

THE LEGAL DIVORCE: The legal divorce is about settling the issues of property, children and support, and the paperwork and red tape you go through to get your Judgment. No matter what your legal divorce is like, no matter what you do or how you do it, you will find your route through the legal divorce on this map. The legal divorce is far simpler than you may have been led to believe—you can see that there are only three main routes through it. Whenever there *are* complications in a divorce, they are always on the level of legal rules and red-tape or human relations.

The worst path: Too many people take the blind path where you go into your divorce without any good idea of what a divorce is really all about. You just go uninformed and unprepared to ask some lawyer to get you a divorce and leave your whole life in the lawyer's lap, hoping it turns out well. *This is the worst thing you can possibly do!* Of course, it might work out—and you might win the lottery, too—but success on this path depends almost entirely on dumb luck. The likelihood for unnecessary pain and expensive outcome is quite high.

One important option is not obvious on this map: if you start off on the blind path, it is often possible to get off and get on one of the better routes—but the sooner the better: as you go further along the blind path, it can become harder to get off.

Knowing where you are going: The two better routes both start when you learn about divorce, then work on your best options.

Notice that there are two branches of the better route—for cases that start with the spouses in active disagreement and cases where there is no likelihood of legal opposition from the outset.

Unopposed cases: Cases that are unopposed—where there is no legal opposition, that is—are relatively easy; they tend to go smoothly and can be very inexpensive. If you have this kind of case, you can easily do your own divorce (Chapter 9) with a book or kit, or you can do it with the inexpensive assistance of a paralegal or a divorce typing service.

Cases with disagreement: First, you have to choose—do you want to start by trying to work out an agreement, or do you want to go to a lawyer first and negotiate later. Are you playing hardball or softball? Before you decide, make sure you understand the overwhelming advantages, both financial and emotional, of an agreed divorce over a contested battle. Don't go to an attorney without becoming informed and prepared first.

If your spouse is being bad or playing hardball, go straight to the best tough attorney you can find (Chapter 11) to take protective action. Try to avoid being rushed into an uncontrolled battle. If you *are* forced to take immediate action, read this book, get informed and take more control as soon as you can.

Most people will choose to work very hard to reach an agreement because it is worth it. You can help yourself a lot by learning conflict reducing techniques and, if you want to, you can get a lot of good help from counseling and mediation. But some people will decide they don't even want to try—they'd rather not deal with their spouse or their life that way. Either way, if you don't try for agreement or if you try and nothing works, the worst thing that can happen is that you end up in a controlled battle, and that is a whole lot better than an uncontrolled battle.

Controlled battle: This is what happens if you decide not to work toward an agreement or if you have tried and can't reach one. A controlled battle is a legal contest conducted with lawyers, but you know exactly what is going on. The issues of disagreement are well defined, and *you* are the one calling the shots. The worst outcome on this side of the map is far better and cheaper than what you are likely to get from going into things uninformed and unprepared.

Finding your way

Now that you've had your bird's—eye view of the terrain, take a look at these general directions for finding your way to a better divorce.

One: Study the territory. Learn how to deal with the real divorce in Chapter 3 and how to take care of business in Chapter 4. Chapter 6 tells you what the legal divorce is about and what you can get from the law, while Chapter 7 explains how you can avoid the incredible disadvantages of the legal system.

Two: Get organized and get prepared. Learn how to do structured problem solving in Chapter 3. Clarify your interests, decide what you want. Use the worksheets in Chapter 5 to start preparing your case and yourself.

Three: Think about turning your case into one that is either settled by agreement or at least without legal opposition—then you can easily get an inexpensive divorce either by doing it yourself or with the help of a divorce typing service (or paralegal).
   • Chapter 9 is about handling cases where there is no legal opposition. No matter how much conflict you have, you should read about unopposed cases to help you understand the advantages of agreement.
   • Chapter 8 is about cases with disagreement or conflict. Learn about the various ways you can reduce conflict and avoid a battle. Try to agree, or at least agree to disagree peacefully.

Four: If you face extreme conflict, or someone is playing hardball, or if you can't (or don't want to) avoid a battle, Chapter 10 is about how to wage and win a *controlled* battle—one where *you* are in charge and where you learn to fight effectively and to minimize the cost and damage.

Five: Learn how to pick the professional advisers you will use. Choosing a counselor or mediator is discussed in Chapter 8. Chapter 11 explains how to choose and how to use a lawyer to your best advantage.

The Real Divorce is Free

The state of your emotions has great *practical* significance. In order to make sound practical decisions—indeed, to solve any of your problems—you need to be very aware of your inner condition and, often, that of your spouse. You need to know how to deal with emotional issues and especially how not to get stuck in psychological traps. Understanding some basic things about how the real divorce works will help you enormously in dealing with yourself, your spouse and your list of practical problems.

This chapter and the next are about what we call the real divorce, with practical information and advice to help you get through it. The real divorce is about ending one life and beginning another, then making it work—spiritually, emotionally and practically. The real divorce is about making a new life and seeking a new center of balance.

Possibly the most real thing in your life right now is the way you feel. Nothing else in your life is as real as your pain, fear, anger, hurt, guilt, tension, nervousness, illness, depression—whatever it is you are feeling. The practical tasks you face are also very real: how to get by financially, how to rearrange the parenting of your children, what to say to family and friends, what to do next, and so on. The real divorce, then, presents these challenges:

Emotional: This is about breaking (or failing to break) the bonds, patterns, dependencies, and habits that attach you to your ex-spouse—learning to let go of anger, fear, hurt, guilt, blame, and resentment. You learn about past mistakes so you don't have to repeat them; you develop a balanced view of yourself, your ex-spouse, and your marriage; you create self-confidence and an openness to new intimate relationships.

Physical: Our minds and bodies are *not* separate and life does *not* come in these neat boxes. Emotions—especially strong ones that are ignored, denied or repressed—are frequently expressed physically. During divorce, people tend to experience a lot of tension and nervousness, they get ill frequently and have accidents. This is a time when you must take extra good care of your health, pay close attention to your body, and be extra careful when driving.

Practical: This is about taking care of business on the physical plane—including the legal divorce. It's the nuts and bolts of what to do, where to go, how to get there as you begin to build a new life for yourself. You need to create safety and security for yourself and your children; to make ends meet in a new life-style that produces what you need and needs no more than you can produce.

In contrast to the real divorce, the legal divorce is specifically about peace, property, custody and support. It is a ritual ceremony that you are required to go through. What you end up with is a bit of paper with court orders written on it. So, what does the legal divorce accomplish for you and what does it have to do with the real divorce? Surprisingly little, as you will see; it is just a sub-category of the practical real divorce. But the legal divorce *does* have important symbolic value. When you file those papers, it makes an important statement to your spouse, to yourself and to the world that a decision has been made, that a new identity and a new direction has been chosen. In practical terms, it forces you to deal with at least a few of your important practical issues (property, custody and support). That's about it for the legal divorce.

The real divorce is what your life is about and how you go about it—it is your real work in life. And unless you decide to get counseling or go into therapy, the real divorce doesn't cost a dime. It is, however, very costly in terms of personal effort, but here, too, you can reduce the cost by learning to avoid the common traps. Going through major life changes—in other words, re-creating your life—is demanding, painful, hard work, but it may be the most important thing you can do.

Before discussing the problems and solutions of the real divorce, here's a very practical method you can use to organize and solve *all* of your problems.

People going through divorce tend to have more accidents, so be extra careful in everything you do.

22

Of course, you should live your life whatever way seems right and best for you, but whenever you don't know what else to do, there's always this method to come back to.

Briefly, what you do is organize your divorce into a list of problems that you keep re-arranging in order of immediacy and importance. Then, from time to time you work on thinking up possible solutions and alternatives for each item, dealing with the most pressing problems first. Even emotional and life problems can be organized and solved this way, but the easiest to pinpoint will be the legal and practical ones. Just structure that part and you'll be way ahead. This method helps you to see exactly what you have to deal with and it makes the unknown take shape and become manageable.

First things first: The order in which you want to solve problems will, in general, follow the hierarchy developed by psychologist Abraham Maslow. He said that people have to satisfy their needs in this order:
  • Physiological needs—hunger, thirst, fatigue.
  • Safety—shelter, avoidance of pain and anxiety, general physical security.
  • Need to belong and feel loved—affection, intimacy, family and friends.
  • Esteem—need for self-respect, a sense of competence.
  • Self-actualization—to be fully what you can be; to explore knowledge, curiosity, aesthetics.
When a lower need is unsatisfied, he said, all behavior tends to be directed to fulfilling it. If satisfaction is a recurring or continual problem, all the higher levels will fail to develop properly. You can use Maslow's hierarchy to help guide the priority of items on your list of problems.

For example, when hurt, any dumb animal knows enough to crawl into a den or a nest and just lay still and heal. People are smarter than animals (we are told) but they don't always know enough to hole-up, get very quiet and heal. Divorce can cause deep physical and emotional injury, so in the early stages of divorce, the first and most important thing you can do is to create *temporary* physical safety and security for you and any children in your custody. You need a place where, for a while, you can feel safe and a period of time to be relatively quiet, and relatively free of pressure and distraction.

What you are after *at first* are short-term solutions—think of weeks or a few months, not years. Don't try to solve all of your problems at once or create solutions that will last forever. Just take care of immediate needs, create a space for healing, and put the rest off until you have had some time to heal. Most of your problems will wait until you are ready to face them.

When you feel relatively clear and ready to start dealing with your life, begin to make a list of problems that you have to solve. Like this:

• Write down your thoughts on index cards as you read through this book. Rework your list as your understanding improves. Turn it into a diary or journal if you like.

• For each problem, make notes on additional information you need to get and resources you can use to help in the solution.

• As you work with your list, keep numbering and re-numbering the items in order of priority. Put your most urgent and most important problems at the top.

• Write down your ideas for possible solutions. Talk to your friends and family. Get ideas for solutions from this book, check out local family services and divorce support groups, or seek advice from professionals.

• Especially in the early stages, don't try for a final resolution of problems that can wait. Seek short-term and temporary solutions whenever possible. Don't do any long-term planning until your life settles down and you begin to see more clearly and calmly. Be sure to take frequent vacations from problem-solving so you can relax.

• Now for the most important part: be sure to balance your list of problems with a similar list of resources you can use and things you have to be grateful for. Write down your material and personal resources: assets, friends and family, health, job, and so on. Concentrate on your strengths: curiosity, love of life and people, your desire to grow and improve.

If you do things this way, you will begin to see what you have to deal with. The whole confusing mess will have turned itself into a relatively short list of problems and each will have a variety of possible solutions. You may not be able to solve all of your problems immediately; few people can, but all you can ask of yourself is that you do your best with what you've got.

In scientific studies of life's most stressful events, divorce always comes in at the very top. Those-who-leave have different emotions from those-who-get-left, but the degree of turmoil is about the same. The important thing about upset is not *if* you are going to have it but *how* you are going to go through it.

How you go through your divorce is an expression of who you are. The way you deal with your problems will also determine who you will be when the divorce is long over and done with. "As the twig is bent, so grows the tree." You are creating your own future with every thought, word, and act.

Upset in divorce may range from mild to violent; it may feel like you've been physically torn—major surgery without anesthetic—or hit in the head, or just simply gone mad. Upset may last for weeks or it may linger for months, even years. *You can't rush things,* but you *can* avoid getting stuck in the common traps discussed below.

Your experience is unique—no two divorces are the same, but most people experience the same four stages in the recovery process. This is how human beings are built:

1. Shock: The first two stages might be so intense and disorienting that you feel literally insane, wondering if you can cope. Yet everything happens at once and you have no choice—you *must* cope, and you will. You might experience symptoms of shock, such as pain, numbness, feeling out of control or going crazy, loss of concentration, insomnia, extreme eating patterns. You may have wide swings in emotions. Intense anxiety, panic, anger, rage, depression may alternate with interludes of clarity, elation, optimism—and then back again. The shock stage can last from days to several months. It can be frightening and painful but it is *absolutely natural*.

The danger at this stage is getting stuck in denial and numbness, turning your effort to avoid pain and anxiety into a way of life. You *have* to feel, you *have* to grieve and hurt. Don't escape into drink or drugs; just let it happen. Trying to deny or avoid or run from the experience will only make it last longer. The depth of your pain is also the measure of your capacity for love and joy.

2. Rollercoaster: After the shock stage, the intensity tends to subside, perhaps become intermittent—this is the main difference from the shock stage—but you get confusing swings in emotions, especially your feelings for your mate and for yourself. You feel like you can't trust your feelings. Almost any little thing can set you off—a smell, a song, a memory. You dwell on the past, constantly reliving it and evaluating. You may feel guilt, blame, self-blame, anger, shame, loss, loneliness, or depression. The way you think about yourself is shaky and uncertain; you feel incompetent, awkward, inadequate, unlovable. Your feelings go around and around and around; they seem to never settle down.

This is all very natural, part of the grieving process, part of letting go of the past, and very necessary. It can go on for a few months to a year. You are under high stress and may be prone to illness and accident, so you have to take extra good care of yourself. Divorce is very much like recovering from major surgery. A big piece of your life has been removed. Be patient, be kind; pamper yourself a little.

Your judgment is likely to be poor while you are in this state, so try to avoid making important decisions. Unfortunately, this is exactly when you have to deal with your divorce and create new arrangements for your children. Put off making permanent decisions if possible; try instead for temporary solutions. Whenever decisions are necessary, try to make them during your calm interludes. Try not to be rash or impulsive. When in doubt, consult with trusted family and friends or stick to established standards such as those set by law. The middle of the road is safest on dark streets.

The mistake you want to avoid here is getting stuck. Your feelings are valid, but don't make a career of them. If you find

that you are going around and around on the same themes, you will eventually have to stop spinning your wheels and wasting time.

If you dwell on loss, blame, or being wronged, you will prolong your own depression, anger, or fear. Don't get stuck too long—you need to get on with your life. Get out of your past and into your future.

3. Self-development: *Divorce is over when the end becomes a beginning.* The rollercoaster eventually evens out more and more. Now you begin to notice the possibilities of your new life. The present and the future become more important than the past. You pay a lot of attention to yourself and your image. You make plans. You make new friends, experiment with new interests and experiences. You may act like a kid again. Dating and sex may bring on a certain degree of confusion, a re-run of old feelings from as far back as adolescence. Have fun discovering what you are, who you are and who you like—but don't overdo it.

4. Emergence: You are getting comfortable with yourself, getting stronger, increasingly clear and aware of who you are. You are more interested in the present and the future. You have a new center of balance as a single person, whole and complete to yourself, and you are now ready for intimacy in new relationships. You survived the divorce and have been strengthened by it. You can still feel grief and sadness about the past, but without guilt, blame or resentment. You are no longer threatened by your own feelings.

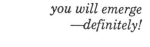

If you don't get stuck, you will emerge —definitely!

Remember that your spouse is going through these cycles, too. Whatever anger and grief your spouse is experiencing is helping to break the bonds of attachment. It is a necessary part of the healing process.

Let's take a look now at some of the major emotional components of the divorce cycle.

Pain: You have to recognize that pain is not only natural, it can be a helper and a good adviser. Especially at first, pain may only mean that you have been injured and are healing, as if you had broken your leg or suffered a grievous wound. But at other times it can be a message that something is wrong, that you have to pay attention to something you have been ignoring. The intensity of pain during divorce can be frightening, but you mustn't run from it or try to block it out or avoid it. To do so will delay your healing or even leave you permanently impaired in spirit. Instead, embrace it; let it happen. The pain is in your heartspace and that is where the real "you" lives, so it is calling you home to your center and to your real self. Endure your suffering, accept your pain and listen to it. If you do, it will run its course and heal more quickly; it will lead you to your solutions; it will provide the energy for your changes and growth; it will make you stronger.

Fear: The major challenge in any divorce is to deal constructively with your fear. Fear of pain, fear of hurt, fear of the future, fear of your ability to take care of yourself and your children, fear of losing self-respect, fear of fear. There is a basic bewilderment of life when so much is happening that you feel you can't possibly cope; you just don't know what to do or how to live. Fear is the root source of anger. Anger is the flip-side of fear. Anger turned inward is depression.

Anger: Learning how to use anger constructively is one of the most important lessons to be gained from your divorce. Anger is a potent source of energy and a very useful emotion *if* you know how to use it. Anger helps get you through the first and most painful stages of divorce by providing an outlet for inexpressible emotions and it helps break the bonds of affection and attachment.

For people who have never shown it, learning how to get angry is a huge step forward. Anger will help you to stop being dependent, stop being a victim. Anger and action are far better than making a career of being depressed, downtrodden, and helpless. You *can* learn to be angry, assertive and constructive all at the same time.

On the other hand, some people become addicted to anger and they misuse it badly. Anger soon becomes self-defeating and self-destructive; the cause of bad mistakes in judgment (like running to a lawyer before you are prepared) that will work against your own interests. Anger can drag you into an uncontrolled battle.

The attraction of anger is that it is cheap and easy—easier than actually solving your real problems; easier than taking responsibility for your own life. It is reliable, always there; you can count on it. For just a moment, it gives you a false sense of power and control; it lets off your steam. But anger is a solution that solves nothing. It serves only to distract you from having to face your own pain, fear or guilt. If you abuse anger, if you become a habitual user, it will poison your life and turn you into an unhealthy, lonely, bitter, spiteful person. You can count on it.

If anger is a personal issue for you and you want to learn to use it well, you will find some good reading on the subject listed in the Appendix. If anger and conflict are a major problem in your divorce, turn to Chapter 8 to read about techniques for reducing the level of conflict. For cases with extreme conflict, read Chapter 10.

Hurt: It is a painful and terrible thing to be hurt by someone you depend on, someone you love and trust. In the early stages of divorce, you may need to heal from hurt that you have experienced, but you do *not* need to continue allowing yourself to be hurt. Someone can hurt you only if you give them the power to do so. Hurt then becomes something that you do to yourself, something you permit to happen. Staying hurt long after the divorce is over keeps you stuck on your needs and weaknesses; it reinforces your picture of yourself as a victim.

Healing

Healing starts with a lot of very little changes in your daily habits. If you take charge of the little things, the big ones will soon fall in line. You must see it as a triumph when you learn to do for yourself the little things that you always depended on your spouse to do, or make decisions in areas where you always used to defer to your mate. Take pleasure in your new self–reliance when you learn to cook, take care of business, grow house plants, remember birthdays, mow the lawn, create an enjoyable living space, or keep the checkbook balanced. When you change your daily habits in the small ways, you are on your way up.

One of your great healing strengths is whatever it is that got you this far in this book—your curiosity, your desire to know things, a desire to take control of your life. Think about your other strengths and advantages.

Gratitude: Another major healing force—one of the most important—is gratitude. This is something you can work on intentionally. Focus on the things in your life that are right at least as much and as often as you dwell on problems. Several times each day, take the time to get quiet inside yourself and think about all the things that you have to be grateful for. Make a list; try to develop a strong sense of gratitude for your life and its many blessings.

Self-reliance: Getting divorced means that you will no longer let your mate's moods and actions dominate your life. You are disentangling yourself from all the old patterns that didn't work for you. You can't control your spouse, but you *can* start to control your own actions. Learn not to react to your spouse's bad conduct and not to push back when your own buttons get pushed. Take responsibility for your own feelings, for your own life.

Acceptance and forgiveness: Possibly the most effective way to speed the healing process—the best way to achieve your own health and balance—is to completely accept your loss, feel your pain, and try to forgive your ex-mate and yourself. Guilt and blame are heavy burdens that can only hold you back and drag you down. Not forgiving keeps you stuck in a view of yourself as a victim. For your own sake, let it all go. Letting go is very different from repressing. You can't heal properly if you deny, avoid or repress your feelings—to the contrary, you want to feel your pain and loss. If you accept your feelings, they will run a natural, healing course; then you can forgive, let go of the past and get on with your life. Read more about forgiveness in books listed in the Appendix.

Support: Make an effort to seek out and use the help and comfort that is available from people in your life. You need the support of friends and family. If you can get it, use it. You can also get a lot of help from family services organizations, divorce support groups and single parent support groups. Make the effort to contact them; it may be very valuable and you have nothing to lose. For references, call your local social services or human resources agency or the local courthouse clerks. You can also get references

Get ahold of yourself!

to support groups in your area through a local church or temple. If one group isn't what you want, try another. Then, there's the professional support that you can get from working with a good counselor. Chapter 8 discusses how to choose a counselor.

In divorce, your emotional problems (looking backward) often disguise a great opportunity (looking forward). As Nietzsche said, taking a hard line, "That which does not kill us makes us strong." Another way to look at it is that you can learn a lot about what is really important in life and what your goals really are. At the very least, you need to learn not to create the same old patterns, not to repeat the same mistakes.

30

Pain is natural and unavoidable when you separate, but people have many ways of unwittingly increasing their pain and prolonging it. A lot of your pain may be entirely unnecessary.

Most unnecessary pain is caused by a very bad habit—negative thinking. There are self-defeating thought patterns that keep you stuck in anger, anxiety or depression. Whether aware of it or not, people are almost continually describing the world to themselves, and it's that quiet, constant voice that forms your attitude—your pre-disposition to experience things negatively. Don't be too quick to decide that you don't do this—it is so habitual that you may not even be conscious of it. That's what makes it hard to cope with.

Negative thinking causes you to paint your life in black with too broad a brush. The way you see things will be one-sided, overly-simple and unbalanced. Negative thinking keeps you boxed in, limits your possibilities, keeps you from seeing solutions and prevents you from moving forward with your life. What you think turns into what you feel. If you expect the worst, that may be what you get. Here are some classical examples of negative thinking:

• **Over-generalizing** is when you think or say things like, "You *always* put me down," or "I'll *never* find another mate," or "She *only* wants one thing from me." You have picked on one negative feature and made it into your total understanding. Try to stop using words like all, always, every, never, only, and totally, and so on.

• **Labeling** would be, "He's a selfish person," or "She's a bitch," or "I'm a loser." You pick on one negative quality and let that represent the whole person. This keeps you angry at others and disgusted with yourself.

• **Blame**-of-self and blame-of-others makes it seem as if the fault for your misfortune is all one-sided, but life is never like that and blame has unfortunate side-effects. If you blame yourself, you are trapped in guilt. If you blame your spouse, you make yourself a victim, avoid your own responsibility, and prolong your anger. That's all over now; the fact is that you each made your own choices and are responsible for your own actions. Now, get on with your life.

The real divorce is free

• **Filtering** happens when you see only the negative or threatening side of things. Focusing on your fears and losses will keep you in a state of anxiety or depression.

• **Catastrophizing** is when you exaggerate potential threats and stay focused on *anticipated* harm or disaster. "I'll never be able to pay my bills." "I can't survive this pain and loneliness." You expect the worst and don't expect to cope.

To avoid the consequences of negative thinking, you have to become more aware of your inner voices and attitudes. Try to notice when you are scaring yourself or seeing things through an all-black filter. When you catch yourself at it, stop. When the negative thoughts start again (and they will), catch them again. Keep at it. Don't be self-critical and put yourself down; just observe and be patient. Give yourself a little reward each time you catch yourself— a cookie or a balloon. Don't laugh, it works. Make yourself think in a more constructive vein: concentrate on solutions instead of problems, think about past pleasures, fantasize about future ones. Try to make yourself take a more balanced and rounded view of things. Stop and breathe, take a walk. Go get some flowers; make your space nice. Keep your attention focused only on things you can see, touch or smell.

This is very hard work and it takes a long time. Don't put yourself down if you don't succeed over-night. You can get a lot of help from a good counselor with this kind of work.

Basic elements of a successful divorce

Experience and academic studies have helped us identify the basic elements of a successful emotional divorce. "Successful," as used here, means completing the process of emotional separation, reaching a new center of balance as a single person, maintaining the welfare of your children, and establishing healthy attitudes toward yourself, your ex-spouse, and your past marriage.

Absence of conflict is *not* part of the ideal divorce. A degree of anger and conflict is natural, useful, even constructive. It helps to break the bonds of attachment and old patterns of relationship; it makes you think and reflect; it makes you change. But *excessive* and *destructive* conflict requires special treatment. The discussion of conflict and how to deal with it is in Chapter 8.

Apart from peace of mind, growth and other human values, there are very practical advantages to struggling as hard as you can to make your divorce better. The closer you can get to the ideals discussed below, the more you will ease tensions and conflict; you will have a far greater chance for compliance with terms of any agreements; you will save thousands in legal costs; if you have children, you will greatly improve co-parenting and cooperation. In short, everything works better.

BASIC ELEMENTS OF A SUCCESSFUL DIVORCE

Mutuality: Lack of mutual sharing in the decision to divorce is the primary cause of conflict in the divorce and post-divorce periods. In an ideal divorce, the decision is arrived at together. This does not mean that one spouse may not be sadder or more distressed than the other, but that both come to accept divorce as the best thing under the circumstances. The spouses should be mutually active in negotiating terms and in co-parenting. The most stable settlements occur when both spouses take an active role in the negotiations, not simply leaving it to a lawyer. A good divorce is an actively mutual enterprise.

Attitude: Each spouse should end up with a balanced view of the other spouse and of the marriage experience. There should be a sense of emotional and spiritual closure. You should be free of any lingering feeling of blame, guilt or failure. You want to create increased self-understanding, the ability to form healthy new intimate relationships, and a sense of self-confidence.

Children: In an ideal divorce, injury to children is minimized, primarily through maintaining good co-parenting relations. Children can literally be destroyed by fighting between their parents, so it is *very* important that parents be able to work together for the well-being of their children. When not resolved, conflict can go on for years, even after the legal divorce is over. *Children must be free of the feeling that loving one parent is a betrayal of the other.* They must be free of the thought that they are the cause of the divorce.

Trying to create the ideal divorce is like any other ideal you try to achieve, like ideal health or achievement in some sport. Your goals are something you work toward, but you don't want to beat yourself up every time you fall short. Just try your best. The closer you can get, the better and smoother your divorce will go, and the better your future will be.

Rules of the road for getting through a tough time

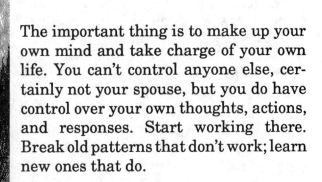

The important thing is to make up your own mind and take charge of your own life. You can't control anyone else, certainly not your spouse, but you do have control over your own thoughts, actions, and responses. Start working there. Break old patterns that don't work; learn new ones that do.

You have to do the inner work yourself. You can get help from professional counselors or friends or books, but in the final analysis you have to look inside for answers to life's problems. Whether you discover your own answers or borrow the best advice you can find from wherever you can find it, the choice—and the task—is yours.

Here, on the next two pages, are some rules of the road for the divorce journey. These are adapted from material developed by Sharon Baker for use in her family counseling practice in Rancho Palos Verdes, California.

Rules of the Road #1 —
Getting Yourself Through a Tough Time

1. You can expect to go through a cycle of
   - shock and denial
   - anger/depression
   - understanding and acceptance.

Then it goes around and around—many times—between anger/depression and acceptance. After a time, acceptance becomes stronger and lasts longer.

2. Let your attention focus on your loss; it is a good way to understand your pain. There is a message in your pain that will lead to solutions. Pain can give you motivation and energy to bring about changes.

3. Seek quiet and rest. Take extra good care of yourself. Exercise, eat properly, keep life as simple as possible.

4. Acknowledge and express your feelings. Talk to someone who knows how to listen. Keep a journal.

5. Seek out support from friends, family, clergy, divorce or crisis support groups, counselors.

6. Stay aware. Do not try to alter or numb your feelings with substances, such as alcohol, drugs, or overeating.

7. Be realistic in what you expect from yourself. It is normal to have mood changes, to feel confused, to have mixed feelings about your spouse.

8. Have faith in your beliefs and in yourself. Remember to be grateful for what you *do* have. Having life, you are a miracle of creation. You are alive, you can feel, you can learn, you can grow.

9. Work. Enjoy the benefits of a daily schedule and of accomplishment, especially in the small changes you are gradually adding to your life to make it better.

10. Be good to yourself.

11. Take time to be with adults and to enjoy social activities when you are ready.

12. Remember that healing is already in process. Time and nature are on your side. You *will* recover!

Rules of the Road #2 —
Getting Your Children Through a Tough Time

1. Tell children the truth in simple terms with simple explanations. Tell them where their other parent has gone.

2. Reassure them that they will continue to be taken care of and that they will be safe and secure.

3. Your children will see that parents can stop loving each other. Reassure them that a parent's love for a child is a special kind that never stops.

4. Spend time with each child individually. Whether you have custody or visitation, the most important thing to the child is your individual relationship with that child. Build the best relationship you can in your circumstances. The future is built of many tiny moments.

5. Children may feel responsible for causing the divorce. Reassure them that they are not to blame. They may also feel that it is their responsibility to bring their parents back together. Let them know that your decision is final and will have to be accepted.

6. Often divorcing parents feel guilty and become over-indulgent. Give your child love, but also give limits.

7. Your child is still a child and can't become the man of the house or a little mother. Continue to be a parent to your child. Seek other adults to fill your own need for companionship.

8. Avoid situations that place a child in the impossible position of choosing between parents:
   - Don't use your child as a way to get back at your spouse. Children can be terribly wounded when caught in a cross-fire.
   - Don't say anything bad about the other parent in hearing of a child.
   - Don't say or do anything that might discourage the child from spending time with the other parent.
   - Don't encourage a child to take sides.

9. You and your former spouse will continue to be the parents of your children for life. Pledge to cooperate responsibly toward the growth and development of your children as an expression of your mutual love for them.

10. Be patient and understanding with your children. Be patient and understanding with your self.

4

Taking Care of Business

The business end of divorce is about what you own and what you are going to live on in the future—your assets, debts, investments, cash flow, budgeting and taxes.

Divorce is an important financial event—perhaps the most important one of your life. The way you resolve your financial settlement, the choices and decisions you make now, can influence your financial well-being for the rest of your days.

Divorce is a time when you have to learn to take care of yourself, and you really do have to take care of business. This is where it starts. Try to spend *at least* as much time focused on business as you do on your emotional issues. Try very hard to keep business and emotional issues entirely separate.

In order to take control of your own life and make sound financial decisions about your divorce, you have to know what you want. In order to negotiate you have to know what you want. In order to tell your attorney what to do, you have to know what you want. The only way to figure out what you want is to know the facts and understand them. Then you have to know what both you and your spouse are entitled to by law (Chapter 6). Then you can make sound decisions about what you want.

First, gather facts and documents. Use the worksheets discussed in Chapter 5 to help you organize and understand your information. After you have all the information available, if you still don't understand your affairs, get help from an accountant, a credit counselor, a financial counselor or an attorney. Go over your facts with them until it all makes sense.

Knowledge is power. With it, you have strength and control. Without it you are helpless, a victim. Often, one spouse has more information and therefore more negotiating power than the other.

If there is an imbalance in bargaining power and strength between you and your spouse, the situation can be greatly improved with knowledge and information.

Your goals for the immediate future are to:
• gather facts, organize and understand all the financial aspects of your joint lives (Chapter 5);
• understand your rights and obligations (Chapter 6);
• decide what you want;
• plan how to live on your new income in a changed life-style.

To get through your divorce, you will need to know all the facts and have all relevant documents in order, both for your own understanding and for your attorney, if you use one. If you get properly prepared ahead of time, you will have more peace of mind and you can save yourself thousands of dollars.

Common traps

Ignorance is the most common trap in the business of divorce. Because your life is upside down, you may not want to deal with tedious financial details, but if you don't take the trouble to understand what's going on in your own financial life and what you are entitled to, you might as well hang a big "victim" sign around your neck. Ignorance increases your own sense of helplessness and leaves you vulnerable to the risk of being manipulated, of getting a bad deal. You can seek advice and assistance from professionals, but you should never rely on anyone but yourself to take care of your business for you. Use the worksheets in this book to organize and understand your own business.

Bad judgment is a real hazard when emotions are running high, but let's face it, divorces are like that. Insecurity makes you doubt your own thinking and ability. Fear and anger make you grasp for too much or surrender too much. Of course, you should get what you are entitled to, but to demand more for emotional reasons is inviting a ruinous conflict that might leave you with less in the end. Giving up what you have a right to can leave you with a future full of regret if not hardship. So be careful and take precautions against your own emotionally affected judgment:

• Understand the emotional cycles that *both* you and your spouse are going through (Chapter 3). Keep in mind that at any given time, emotions can strongly affect your judgment and decision–making ability.
• Keep business and emotional issues separate (see below).
• Don't jump to sudden conclusions or make impulsive agreements or decisions. Above all, unless you face a desperate emergency that can't wait, don't rush off to a lawyer until you have some information and get yourself prepared.
• Don't sign anything you haven't thought about or don't understand.
• Keep a journal and make entries in it regularly about your thoughts and feelings. Keep track of your evolving priorities, possible solutions to problems, and your goals. Review your journal regularly, especially before making any final decisions.
• Use the law as a guide. You are not required to follow the legal standards, but they have been worked out over millions of cases, so if you are confused or in doubt about what you want to do, and if the laws in your state are clear and predictable, use them as a guide.
• Seek advice from reliable, informed, experienced people.

Excessive spending is very common before, during and after a separation. At first, spending seems like a denial of the growing distance and disaffection between the spouses. A couple will buy a new home or remodel their old one, buy a car, take a long vacation, have a baby—anything to bring them together in something. This is not usually consciously planned, it just works that way. During separation, spending is used as an anesthetic for emotional pain. After separation, the couple genuinely needs a lot of money to set up two separate life-styles, added to which is neurotic spending driven by emotional upset.

Being aware of this trap may be of some help, but it is often difficult to see and control your own eccentricities. Control impulsive and compulsive buying the same way you would control neurotic eating habits. The best thing is to take every possible step to keep yourself open, centered and strong. Deal directly with your emotional issues instead of reacting and running from them.

Money–hiding is not common but it is not rare, either. Sometimes, when it becomes clear that a divorce is coming, one spouse or the other will start salting money away in a private money stash. If done without cheating the community, this is actually a good idea because it gives that spouse a sense of security, independence and control. However, if *marital* assets (that belong to both spouses) are being secretly diverted into a separate account, this is a clear case of cheating. In moderate amounts, it may not be worth fighting over, but it is something to watch out for, keep track of, and include in any future accounting. In extreme cases, you will want an attorney to take emergency measures to protect the marital estate and your interest in it.

Sometimes, the money manager will spend joint savings or take out a loan for living expenses while putting regular income into a separate account. A family business can be manipulated or run into the ground so income appears low later. Or bonuses and commissions can be postponed until after separation. The list is almost endless.

If a divorce is coming, take a careful look at plans to refinance your house or other kind of loan. Watch where income goes and watch your savings account withdrawals. After separation, take a close look at financial transactions during the previous year.

Keep business and personal matters separate

Divorce has a lot of business–like aspects (money, property, negotiation and agreements) and it is widely understood that business and emotions don't mix well. One of the best things you can do for yourself is to decide to keep business and personal/emotional matters separate—or as separate as possible. This will make a big contribution toward reducing the level of conflict and confusion in your case and in your own mind. Be sure to tell your spouse what you have decided to do and explain that it will help you both. You can benefit from taking this step unilaterally, but try to get your spouse to agree; set a good precedent by starting off with an agreement. Here are some guidelines:

• Work hard to decide what you want ahead of time. Postpone decisions on things you are not clear about. Keep a business diary for your thoughts and decisions and review it from time to time, especially before you go to a meeting.

• Be very business–like. Dress for business instead of casually, adopt a professional attitude and tone of voice. Try to see yourself as two separate people—a business professional and an emotional, feeling human being. Be the other person some other time. Postpone meetings if you cannot be relatively calm and thoroughly prepared.

• Discuss business at appointed times and places. Always be prepared with a written agenda of what you want to talk about and check off each item as it gets done. Bring copies of any necessary documents. Take notes.

• If you meet in person, do *not* meet at the home of either spouse. It is too personal, it triggers emotions, and someone may feel at a disadvantage. You should be able to get up and leave if necessary. Meet instead at a coffee–shop, in a library or school meeting room, at a park or a friend's house if it feels good. Anywhere quiet, safe and neutral will do, but do not meet at a spouse's home.

• You should refuse to discuss business and personal matters in the same conversation. Be consistent and diligent about this. If something personal comes up when talking business, say "I'd like to discuss that later with you, please," and offer to set a specific time for it. If your spouse persists, hold firm, repeat your request once more, then explain that you will leave or hang up if it happens again. If necessary, do so. Don't get excited or emotional; be business-like, but stick to your decision.

• Refuse to talk business when you are discussing personal matters. Do not get into a business discussion spontaneously or impulsively. You need to get properly prepared and emotionally composed each time.

• If your spouse is being difficult in your emotional life, try not to let that infect your business relationship. Similarly, if your spouse is being bad in business negotiations, don't let that affect you emotionally. Don't get upset—it's only business.

Money management— two households on one income

This must be the most common of all divorce problems and a powerful source of fear that fuels conflict. Spending needs go up dramatically while income stays stable. If anything, the ability to earn money is reduced during this prolonged crisis, yet two households now have to live on the same old income. It is the unknown that makes us afraid of the future, afraid of change. What will you live on? How will you make ends meet?

Once your physical safety is assured, your next most important need is financial safety. The difference between a desperate existence and a good life is knowing that you have enough coming in and an emergency reserve that will see you through several months. Living securely on a low standard of living is far better than a higher standard of living that is always at risk. Many people don't seem to know that.

Once again, knowledge is power, the ultimate best solution. You will solve your money problems by using a budget to help you understand your situation and to make plans for the future. When the facts are clear, you will know what you have to do to be secure and live in balance.

Here is a seven–point system you can use to solve money problems and plan your future:

• Make an inventory of assets that you own, bills that you owe.
• Study your past spending patterns.
• Make an inventory of income that you can count on.
• Plan your future spending.
• Create a control system.

- Seek creative alternatives and set goals.
- Review and change.

Make an inventory of property that you own and bills that you owe. Use the Assets Worksheet discussed in Chapter 5 to help you organize and analyze your list of assets and debts. Your net worth is the amount by which your assets exceed your liabilities. If you own valuable property after your divorce, you may decide to sell it and use the money for living or for investments. As to debts, any budget you make will have to include a plan to pay them off or discharge them in bankruptcy.

If you find that you are overwhelmed by your debts and repayment makes your budget impossible, you may have to consider plans to reorganize or discharge your debts. Many areas have organizations such as Commercial Credit counselors (see white pages), a non-profit organization that will help you to consolidate and repay your debts. You can also consider discharging debts by declaring bankruptcy. Take a look at the Nolo Press book, "Bankruptcy: Do it Yourself."

Study past spending patterns. Use the Budget Worksheet discussed in Chapter 5 to help you organize and analyze your spending. Gather up all the old records, bills, receipts, checks and checkbook registers you can find covering at least one year. Some expenses are annual or irregular, so a shorter period of time may not give you an accurate picture of annual expenses. If not anticipated, annual expenses (several hundred for insurance, for example) can create a crisis. Offer to make copies of records in your spouse's possession and offer to make copies of records you possess for your spouse to use. If your spouse won't turn over records you need, a lawyer can force them out through a legal process that in most states is called "discovery."

If your records are incomplete, you will just have to make estimates from memory. By all means, start saving checks and receipts from now on and, using the budget worksheet as a guide, keep a precise record of your ongoing expenses over a period of time.

Most people have never analyzed their spending patterns and have never made any organized effort to control their spending. If your income is going to become reduced or uncertain, you may have to start some new habits. Consider it growth, an adventure.

Make an inventory of income that you can count on. Use the Budget Worksheet discussed in Chapter 5. What income can you count on? Naturally, you will need to be very aware of your rights or your obligations regarding child and spousal support. How much can you get? How much will you be expected to pay? What is reasonable? You should also be aware of the possibility that a spouse in need can go immediately into court to ask for temporary support and other orders that will be in effect until a final settlement by agreement or by trial and judgment. Support is discussed in Chapter 6.

You should figure a low estimate for irregular or uncertain income, because if your actual income is low, your planning will fail and you will end up in a financial squeeze. Unfortunately, child support and spousal support (alimony) are, speaking *statistically* about cases in general, an inadequate and unreliable source of income. Spouses who regularly receive the full amount on time are in the minority. Fortunately, the problem has been recognized as a widespread social disaster and laws are getting increasingly aggressive and very tough on people who slack off on their support obligations. But be cautious about how much you figure to rely upon.

Plan your future spending. Now that you know how your money has been spent in the past, you are in a good position to make an informed estimate of spending needs in the future. Again, use the worksheet. You have to make sure that the spending you plan is no greater than the income you can count on.

If you occasionally take in more than you spend, that money should go to emergency reserves and investments for future security. Everyone should try to accumulate enough savings to live on for several months in case of an emergency. That's the only way to be secure.

If your spending needs exceed the income you can count on, you have only two alternatives: reduce your spending needs or find new sources of reliable income. Living on a lower standard of living is much better than the emotional stress and insecurity of living beyond your means. When cutting expenses, the worst place to compromise is in the food category. Your health comes first, but you can live very nicely on fresh fruits and vegetables, grains, and the occasional fish or chicken. Actually, that's the best possible diet, and it doesn't cost as much as packaged foods, fast–foods, and meals out.

If forced to, you can spend your savings or sell off assets to raise money, but these are non–solutions because you aren't solving your basic problem of more going out than comes in. When you run out, then what do you do?

Create a control system. A budget only works if there is some way to keep track of your spending and keep yourself within its guidelines. You don't need to label every penny, but you do want to watch your spending by budget category. There are a variety of methods you can use:

• Sort your income into envelopes by budget category. You can always see what's left to spend in each envelope and when you run out, you're out. The disadvantage is that you may not want to keep loose cash lying around.
• Keeping a ledger book of *everything* you spend is very accurate and works well, but fails if you let down or forget to enter any expenses. This is tedious and requires discipline, but it is the best method in most cases.
• Keep track in your mind. This is simple and works for some people who have simple budgets, but requires discipline and it's easy to make mistakes or fool yourself.
• If you are wealthy, you can hire a financial secretary who receives your income, pays your bills, keeps track of your expenses and gives you a personal allowance.

Seek creative alternatives and set goals. Now that you have a handle on your income and spending, you may want to set some goals for the future. Be as specific as possible. Creating a reserve of emergency funds sufficient for several months should be high on your list. Beyond that, you may want to consider a plan for investing in your future. If your budget is too tight or your income is too low, you will want to try to find ways to create more reliable income. This means looking for new work, more education and training, new opportunities, a new career. Read books on careers and consider seeing a career counselor.

Review and change. After your system runs for a while, you should sit down and review it carefully to see how it is working. Has anything changed? If so, you may need to change your budget. If you can't stay within a category, try to figure out why. Adjust and fine–tune your categories, revise your goals.

Problems? If you find the budget process too complicated or difficult, you may need to see a financial or credit counselor for help and support. Many areas have an office of Consumer Credit Counselors who will either help you or perhaps refer you to someone who can. Otherwise, you might ask your local bank loan manager or an accountant if they know any professionals who specialize in helping people with budgets.

5

Get Organized

Getting reliable information and advice is the best thing you can do to get a better divorce; the next most important thing is being prepared. This means preparing yourself and preparing your case.

Preparing your case means getting the facts of your case clear and organized. The first three of the four worksheets at the end of this chapter are exactly what a good attorney would want to see. Using them will help you get your mind and your information in order; it will help you understand your own case and pinpoint exactly where more information or advice is necessary. If you prepare your case with these worksheets and gather supporting documents before you visit an attorney—*if* you ever do—you will start off saving hours of time and many hundreds of dollars. You will impress the attorney as being well informed and prepared—someone who knows what they are doing.

Preparing yourself includes getting information about divorce, just as you have been doing by reading this book. The real life issues of the real divorce can be very hard to work out and may take a long time to clarify. But in the legal divorce, the issues are much more specific—what do you want to do about property, custody and support? Here's your working method:
- begin to organize your information (Chapter 5);
- learn how divorce works (Chapter 6);
- find out if the laws of your state provide a predictable outcome if the facts in your case were presented in court (Chapter 6);
- the final step of preparation is to decide what you want and how you are going to go about getting it.

Deciding what you want

Deciding what you want requires an understanding of what you are entitled to under the laws of your state and whether or those laws amount to a clearly predictable outcome if your case should end up in court. Then consider what your real values are. Think about what is important to you: security, property, money, revenge, income, peace of mind, your children, cooperative co-parenting, future relationship, doing what's right, being fair, forgiveness, and so on. Then think about what is most important. Attorneys generally work on the premise that getting the most you can is what is important, but you may have different values and you may prefer your values to legal ones. Getting every last cent may not be as important to you as those other things. Or maybe it is.

Getting your hands on the nuts and bolts of your own divorce may appear to be difficult or tedious—something you would rather avoid—but it is *very* important for you to do it. Making your life decisions is not something you can safely or wisely leave to someone else. Besides, even if you get an attorney, you will still have to do this work, and the rewards for dealing with it yourself far outweigh the effort. It is practical, constructive, useful work. It helps you to organize your thinking and it saves you a pile of money and loads of aggravation. It feels good to be in charge of your own life. It is the best way to get the best possible outcome in your case and it gives you an excellent start on your independent new life.

You have to decide how to divide your marital property; how to arrange for the shared parenting of kids, if you have any; and how much support, if any, will be provided for a spouse or children. Maybe your case is very simple or maybe you are already clear about what you want and what's fair. If so, just go right ahead. But in most cases you will want to learn more about what the law would do in your case before you make any final decisions.

Spend some time with the worksheets. Start soon so you can find out how much more you need to find out. Once you have done as much as you can, make a list of questions and information you still need. Read Chapter 6 where we discuss the law and how to learn more about it, and start a list of things you need to find out and decisions you have to make. If you have trouble reaching conclusions, the time has come to get advice. At least you have pinpointed exactly what you need to know. Now you can ask an attorney some very specific questions and get some very specific advice. Do that, then think things over and decide what you want. But make up your own mind—don't live on someone else's values.

Don't make long–term decisions when you are upset; your judgment isn't sound and you don't want to build the rest of your life on decisions based on anger, guilt or fear. Slow things way down and put off making permanent decisions until you are on a more even keel. Try to create short–term, temporary solutions instead of long–term, permanent ones. Be careful that you don't give away too much out of fear, guilt, or just to get it over with; you'll probably regret it later. Be equally careful not to pressure your spouse with guilt or fear. Experience shows that this kind of thing is very likely to backfire later.

Fill out the worksheets

At the end of this chapter you will find four worksheets that will help you organize and analyze your case. Below are some general notes to guide you and notes on the use of each form.

General instructions for all worksheets

• Make two copies of the blank forms before you fill them out so you can have a rough draft, then a final copy. Duplicate your final copy whenever you need to give a copy to a professional who is helping you with your case.

• Put N/A in spaces where the information requested is not applicable to your situation, or put a line through the entire section if it is not relevant; this is so a reader will know that you did not simply forget the item. Put EST where an amount is estimated.

• Pencil in UNK where you don't know the requested information. Keep a list of things you don't yet know. There may be some things you can't find out, but put some effort into digging out information and completing as much of the forms as possible.

• If you run out of room on any item, attach another sheet, put down "continuation of item ___," and continue. When you are completely finished, note the total number of additional pages at the top of the first sheet on the line provided and staple them all together.

THE PERSONAL INFORMATION WORKSHEET

This worksheet and the next are adapted from client intake forms used by attorney Barbara Di Franza of San Jose, California. The first one is quite straight-forward and self-evident. It is useful in any kind of case and should be filled out by everyone.

Notes:

• Items 11, 12, 22, and 23: information about former names is primarily for women who want to take this easy opportunity to have their name legally changed to their maiden name or to a former married name.

• Item 29: if a child does not yet have a social security number, get one. It is important to the enforcement of support orders and necessary for tax exemptions.

• Items 16 and 27 request information on the monetary arrangements with people you and your spouse live with (if any). This is asking if any of the people named are dependents or are otherwise being supported, or if any of them contribute to the household expenses.

THE ASSETS WORKSHEET

If you have any property or bills to divide, you should fill out this worksheet.

Notes:

• You will need to find copies of documents related to any property on this worksheet: deeds, mortgages, trust deeds, notes, registration papers for motor vehicles, serial numbers for major items, account numbers for financial and retirement accounts, and so on. Make copies to hand over if you consult an attorney about your case.

• The value of property is always "fair-market value" which means the amount you can get for the item if sold on the open market less any costs of sale. You will need a professional appraisal for real property, pensions, a going business, or any items of uncertain or disputed value.

• Item 1 (f) and (i) is where you indicate if money for the purchase of the family home came from the separate property of either spouse.

50

• Item 8: "Whole" life insurance has a built in savings plan that builds up cash-in value over time; "term" insurance is cheaper but has no cash-in value. Examine all policies carefully to see which type they are.

• Item 9: For pension plans, in addition to information asked for, you will want to get a "Summary Plan Description" from the administrators of each plan (write to them) and the amount paid in on the account.

Decisions about property

(1) What property is separate? What property is marital and must be divided?

(2) What is the fair-market value of the marital property?

(3) What do I want? How do I want the marital property to be divided?

THE BUDGET WORKSHEET

This should be filled out whenever support for a spouse or child is an issue. You can also use it to help plan how two people can live on the same old income.

The budget can be the hardest of all the worksheets to think through and figure out, but it is probably the most important thing you can do, especially in cases where there is not enough money to live as well as you used to or as well as you would like.

Doing budget work is extremely important and useful because it will help you make decisions about your divorce and make plans and adjustments for your future life-style.

You need to know what both you and your spouse spent in the past and you need to estimate what you will each need to spend in the future. Budgeting your income to pay for two new lives can often be tricky and the source of heated discussion. Do some research on past family records, then give it your very best effort.

After you have done all you can, if you are still having trouble it could be extremely useful to work with a competent financial consultant. To find one, look in the white pages for Consumer Credit Counselors, ask the Better Business Bureau, ask your local bank loan officer, or ask an accountant for references.

• **Note about payments on debts:** These are recorded in three different places. Home mortgage payments are entered at item 1, auto payments at item 6, and all other debt payments go under item 4.

You need to decide
(1) Who needs support?
   —the children? a spouse?
(2) How much support can be afforded?
(3) How to balance fairly between the needs of one and the ability to pay of the other.
(4) How to live on your new income.

PARENTAL ACTIVITY WORKSHEET

This form will help you work out your plans for custody, visitation, and how to share co-parenting. It is adapted from a form devised by Arthur M. Bodin, Ph.D., Diplomate in clinical and forensic psychology, for use in his private practice in Palo Alto, California. Make extra copies of the blank form so both parents can work on it.

The worksheet lists many of the daily chores associated with raising a child, but you will probably want to add more items to fit your own situation. Working through it will help to clarify how you have been sharing the work of parenting in the past and how you plan to do it in the future.

The best thing is for both spouses to fill this one out separately, including estimates or the other spouse's time, then compare notes. It may make you both more realistic about what you will be facing in the

52

future. It can serve as a basis for your discussions on how co-parenting can work.

Go over all the items and indicate with M and F who does what and how often. To be very thorough, estimate the number of hours actually spent per month on each activity and put that number next to each entry in the left column, then add it all up. In the right column, estimate how child-care will work under whatever co-parenting terms are under consideration.

Decisions: Will custody be shared? If not, who will have physical custody and primary responsibility? If one parent gets physical custody, how can parenting be arranged so each parent gets maximum time with the children?

Parenting plans and visitation: In most cases it is best to have your future parenting schedule spelled out in as much detail as possible so everyone knows exactly what to expect and so there are no arguments later. In actual practice, parents can always agree to any arrangements they like at the time, but whenever there are disagreements, a detailed, specific schedule will settle the matter and save a lot of disagreement in the future. Any plan you make can always be changed when you are both in a co-operative mood.

Keep good records

Your work will be easier and go smoother if you are careful to keep your records safe, neat, organized, and all together in one place. Otherwise, you may end up swamped in a mass of papers that will only stimulate your feeling of confusion and frustration. You might misplace important papers. It's easier if you start off right.

Keep file folders in a drawer or box, or go to a stationers and get a large accordion folder with six or more compartments, or just use some large envelopes in a box. Keep a set of files for:

- Correspondence with
    - lawyers
    - spouse
    - others
- Legal Pleadings
- Other Documents
- Worksheets
- Any other categories that will help you sort things out.

Personal information in the marriage of _____

_____
date

There are _____ additional pages attached to this worksheet

ABOUT THE MARRIAGE

1. Date of marriage: _____ Place of marriage: _____
   city   state

2. Date of separation: _____
   (when one of us left the marital bed or at least clearly said the marriage was over)

3. I have resided in this state for _____ years and in the County of _____ for _____ years.
   My spouse resided in this state for _____ years and in the County of _____ for _____ years.

4. The divorce is desired by: ___Husband ___Wife

5. There are _____ children born or adopted into this marriage (further information below)

6. Description of any acts of harassment or violence:
   _____
   _____
   _____

ABOUT MYSELF

7. Name: _____

8. Telephones: Home: (____)_____
   Work: (____)_____ OK to phone at work?_____
   Other: (____)_____ OK to leave message?_____

9. Sex: _____ Age: _____ Date of birth: _____

10. Mailing address:_____
    street   city   state   zip
    Residence address:_____

    County of residence:_____ How long?_____

11. Former name(s): _____

12. ___I do not wish a former name restored.
    ___I want my former name restored as follows: _____

13. Employer: _____

Address: _____
                  street   city   state   zip

Days and times at work: _____

Length of this employment:_____   Approximate monthly gross pay: $_____

There is medical / dental coverage through my employer:

____ for me   ____for my spouse _____for children Monthly cost: $_____   ____ No coverage

My Social Security number:_____ My driver's license number: _____

Cost of child care enabling me to work is $_____ per month.

14. Other sources of income: Approx. amount per month:
    a)_____   _____
    b)_____   _____
    c)_____   _____

15. Health problems for which special attention or care is necessary:
_____
_____

16. Other than my spouse or children, I am currently residing with:

Name	Age	Relationship to me
_____	____	_____
_____	____	_____
_____	____	_____

Monetary arrangements: _____
_____

17. ___I have no will.   ___My most recent will was made on_____.

ABOUT MY SPOUSE

18. Name: _____

19. Telephones: Home: (   )_____
                   Work: (   )_____ OK to phone at work?_____
                   Other: (   )_____ OK to leave message?_____

20. Sex: _____   Age: _____   Date of birth: _____

21. Mailing address:_____
                                street   city   state   zip

    Residence address:_____

    County of residence:_____ How long?_____

22. Former name(s): _____

23. ___Spouse does not wish a former name restored.
    ___Spouse wants former name restored as follows:_____

24. Employer: _____

    Address: _____
                        street   city   state   zip
    Days and times at work: _____

    Length of this employment:_____ Approximate monthly gross pay: $_____

    There is medical / dental coverage through spouse's employer:

       ___ for me ___for my spouse _____for children Monthly cost: $_____ ___ No coverage

    Spouse's Social Security #:_____ Spouse's driver's license #: _____

    Cost of child care enabling spouse to work is $_____ per month.

25. Other sources of income: Approx. amount per month:
    a)_____   _____
    b)_____   _____
    c)_____   _____

26. Health problems for which special attention or care is necessary:
_____
_____

27. Other than our children, my spouse currently resides with:

    Name   Age   Relationship to spouse

_____ ____ _____
_____ ____ _____
_____ ____ _____
_____ ____ _____

    Monetary arrangements with the above persons (known) (suspected):_____
_____

28. Spouse's attorney is:_____
    Address:_____

CHILDREN BORN OR ADOPTED INTO THIS MARRIAGE

29.	Name	Age	Birth date	Soc. Sec. #	Residing with
	_____	___	_____	_____	_____
	_____	___	_____	_____	_____
	_____	___	_____	_____	_____
	_____	___	_____	_____	_____

There (is) (is not) likely to be any dispute about the paternity of any of the children.

30. Special health care problems:_____

_____

_____

31. Income or property owned by any dependent children:

_____

_____

_____

32. Custody and visitation of children:
   a) is currently arranged and is working out as follows:

_____

_____

_____

_____

   b) I want the judgment to order custody and visitation rights as follows:

_____

_____

_____

_____

   c) I anticipate that there (will) (will not) be a dispute over custody and visitation.

MY PREVIOUS MARRIAGES & RELATIONSHIPS

33. I was previously married ____ times before this marriage.

Name of my former spouse(s)	When terminated	How (death, divorce, etc.)
a)_____	_____	_____
b)_____	_____	_____
c)_____	_____	_____

34. Children born or adopted into the previous marriage(s):

Name	Age	Birth date	Residing with
_____	___	_____	_____
_____	___	_____	_____
_____	___	_____	_____

35. Children from a non-marital relationship:

Name	Age	Birth date	Residing with
_____	____	_____	_____
_____	____	_____	_____
_____	____	_____	_____

36. Support paid or received (including any overdue) by me or by the above children, or other income (such as Social Security) received by or on behalf of the above children, is as follows:

_____

_____

_____

_____

MY SPOUSE'S PREVIOUS MARRIAGES & RELATIONSHIPS

37. My spouse was previously married _____ times before this marriage.

Name of former spouse	When terminated	How (death, divorce, etc.)
a)_____	_____	_____
b)_____	_____	_____
c)_____	_____	_____

38. My spouse's children born or adopted into the previous marriage(s):

Name	Age	Birth date	Residing with
_____	____	_____	_____
_____	____	_____	_____
_____	____	_____	_____
_____	____	_____	_____

39. My spouse's children from a non-marital relationship:

Name	Age	Birth date	Residing with
_____	____	_____	_____
_____	____	_____	_____
_____	____	_____	_____

40. Support paid or received (including any overdue) by my spouse or by the above children, or other income (such as Social Security) received by or on behalf of the above children, is as follows:

_____

_____

_____

_____

CURRENT ARRANGEMENTS

41. __We are not yet separated
    __We are separated but have no financial arrangements at this time.
    __We have separated and now live apart under the following financial arrangements:

    Periodic payments (who pays, how much, for what, how often): _____

_____

_____

    Direct payments (Mortgage, bills, et cetera.)

Who pays?	Item	amount	how often paid

    Other arrangements: _____

_____

_____

42. __We have made no written agreements and have no oral understandings.
    __We have a written agreement which is attached.
    __We have oral agreements or understandings as follows: _____

_____

_____

_____

_____

PENDING ISSUES AND QUESTIONS

43. I foresee the following problems in dealing with my spouse (i.e., fear, distrust, dishonesty, unwillingness to compromise, using children as a weapon, violence, et cetera): _____

_____

_____

_____

_____

44. I have some questions and issues I would like to explore, as follows: _____

_____

_____

_____

_____

45. I have already made some decisions about what outcome I would like with respect to property, children, support, or goals and conduct of this case, as follows: _____

_____

_____

_____

_____

Assets in the marriage of _____

Date _____

There are _____ additional pages attached to this worksheet

1. The family home

___We do not own and are not buying the family home (skip to 2.)
___We own or are buying the family home, with an approximate market value of $_____

a) Address:_____
                  street   city   county   state

b) Date of original purchase:_____

c) Title is now in name of ___Husband ___Wife Other: _____

d) Title is held as   ___Joint Tenants   ___Tenants in Common   ___Community Property
        ___Other: _____

    ___Title has been changed since we first acquired it as described here: _____
_____
_____

e) ___We both agree that the house should be divided:
        ___50/50   ___Other: _____

    ___We disagree about the division of the house as follows: _____
_____
_____

    ___There have been ___oral ___written understandings or agreements about ownership of the family home, or about reimbursement for money spent on purchase or improvements (give dates, and details):_____
_____

f) The money for the down payment of $ _____ was provided by:
                       Amount   Source of funds (indicate if separate property used)

___Our joint savings _____   _____
___Husband   _____   _____
___Wife   _____   _____
___Other   _____   _____

g) Money borrowed when home was first purchased:

	Amount	Original Balance	Current Balance
(1) First Deed of Trust	_____	_____	_____
(2) Second Deed of Trust	_____	_____	_____
Later Deeds of Trust	_____	_____	_____

h) __The home was never refinanced.   __The home was refinanced on (date):_____
i) House payments during the marriage were made:
   __entirely from the wages of either spouse.
   __other, as follows (include payments from separate property of either spouse):_____
   _____

2   Other real estate

__Neither spouse owns or is buying any other real estate (skip to 3).
__I or my spouse own the following types of other real estate.
   (Type: R = rental, U = unimproved land, F = farm or ranch, C = commercial property)

	Type	Address	Date purchased	Purchase price	Current Value
a)					
b)					
c)					
d)					

	Amount & source of down pmt.	Balance owed on property	Title in name of H, W, Other	Amount of + or - cash flow per month
a)				
b)				
c)				
d)				

3.   Automobiles

	Registered to	Year	Make	Model	Amount owed	Approx. Miles	Value
a)							
b)							
c)							
d)							

4.   Personal property:
Identify items of special monetary or sentimental value, then lump the rest into general categories such as furniture, appliances, tools, garden equipment, hobby equipment, books, records, sports equipment, paintings, et cetera.

	Description	Value	Amount owing	Who owns it? (H, W, both, other)
a)				
b)				
c)				
d)				
e)				
f)				
g)				
h)				
i)				
j)				
k)				
l)				
m)				
n)				

5. Cash accounts (Checking, saving, credit union, money market, T-bills, certificates of deposit)

In name of H, W, Other	Where held, Type of Acct.	Balance at separation	Balance now	Maturity date	Who controls it? H, W, Other
a)					
b)					
c)					
d)					
e)					

6. Retirement accounts (IRA or Keogh) held by either spouse

In name of H, W, Other	Institution and Branch	Type of Account	Approximate value/ amount	Maturity date
a)				
b)				
c)				
d)				

7. Securities (Mutual funds, bonds, limited partnerships, stocks) owned by either spouse

In name of H, W, Other	Broker (if applicable)	Description (include # of shares, % interest at separation)	Approximate net value
a)			
b)			
c)			
d)			

8. Life insurance policies on either spouse or children

Company	Policy #	Whole or term?	Face Value	Cash value	Beneficiary	Insured
a)						
b)						
c)						
d)						

9. Pension, retirement or profit-sharing benefits in which either spouse *may* have an interest

In name of H or W	Company or Union	Location	Years in plan	Description, amount of benefits
a)				
b)				
c)				
d)				

10. Business interests. Describe any interest held by either spouse in any business, professional practice or corporation, giving approximate value of interest where possible.

_____

_____

_____

_____

_____

11. Tax returns
The last year for which we filed a joint return was _____.
There ___is no tax refund currently due
      ___is still a refund due, $ _____ from the state, $ _____ from the federal government.
Monies owed for previous returns or for returns due to be filed in the next year are as follows: _____
_____
_____

12. Debts

Creditor	Purpose	Balance at separation	Balance today
a)_____			
b)_____			
c)_____			
d)_____			
e)_____			

Part of debt incurred during marriage, before sep.	Annual interest rate	Monthly payment	Written agreement?	Who has records?
a)_____				
b)_____				
c)_____				
d)_____				
e)_____				

13. Education & training:
If marital funds were used for education or training of either spouse that substantially increased that spouse's earning capacity, indicate who for and how much. _____
_____
_____

14. Separate property
   a) If any of the property listed above is separate, make a note in the left-hand margin — "HS" for Husband's separate property, "WS" for Wife's separate property.

   b) List below any other property or debt not listed above that you think is the separate property of either spouse.

Description	How was it acquired	Whose is it?
a)_____		
b)_____		
c)_____		
d)_____		
e)_____		
f)_____		

   c) Note here marital funds or property lost due to gambling. Give dates, amounts, and who lost it.
_____
_____
_____

Budget of _____ **Dated** _____

INCOME

These figures are *gross* earnings per *month*.
Earnings received on other periods are pro-rated to a monthly figure.

	my income	my spouse's income
EARNINGS		
Salary and wages	$	$
Commissions		
INVESTMENT INCOME		
Interest from savings		
Interest from other accounts		
Dividends		
Rental income (gross income less cash expenses; attach schedule)		
Royalties		
OTHER INCOME		
Business profits		
Pensions		
Trusts		
From retirement accounts (IRA, KEOGH)		
Social Security		
Disability & unemployment		
Spousal Support		
Child Support		
Welfare		
Contributions from live-in mates		
Other:		
TOTAL GROSS INCOME	$	$

DEDUCTIONS FROM GROSS INCOME:

- State income tax
- Federal income tax
- Social Security or self-employment tax
- Health insurance
- State disability insurance
- Mandatory pension or retirement deductions
- Mandatory union dues
- Other: (specify)

TOTAL DEDUCTIONS	$	$

NET SPENDING INCOME (Gross less total deductions)	$	$

E X P E N S E S

Expenses are per month.
Payments on other periods are pro-rated to a monthly figure.

FIXED EXPENSES

	our past joint expenses	my future expenses	spouse's future expenses
1. Household			
Rent or mortgage	$	$	$
Property tax			
Telephone			
Gas & Electric			
Water			
Fuel			
Garbage service			
Cable TV			
Other			
Sub total	$ ·	$	$
2. Taxes			
Federal income tax (beyond pg. 1)	$	$	$
State income tax (beyond pg. 1)			
Sub total	$	$	$
3. Insurance			
Life	$	$	$
Health & accident			
Hospitalization			
Fire & Theft			
Personal Property			
Sub total	$	$	$
4. Payments on debts			
Furniture	$	$	$
Appliances			
Charge accounts			
Credit cards			
Personal loans			
Christmas / Chanukkah club			
Other			
Other			
Sub total	$	$	$

	our past joint expenses	my future expenses	spouse's future expenses

5.   Education for self & kids
Tuition $ $ $
Room & board
Books
Other
_____   _____   _____

        Sub total $ $ $

6.   Transportation
Auto payments $ $ $
Auto insurance
Auto license
Parking
Commuting to work
Other
_____   _____   _____

        Sub total $ $ $

7.   Personal allowance
Self $ $ $
Child(ren)
Music lessons
Support for parents
Other dependents
_____   _____   _____

        Sub total $ $ $

8.   Memberships
Union (beyond amount on page 1) $ $ $
Professional associations
Clubs
Religious
Other
_____   _____   _____

        Sub total $ $ $

        Total fixed expenses $ $ $

FLEXIBLE EXPENSES

9.   Food
Groceries $ $ $
Meals out (includes school lunches)
_____   _____   _____

        Sub total $ $ $

10.   Household expenses
Cleaning materials $ $ $
Small home items
Yard care
House cleaning
House maintenance
Repairs
New appliances
New furniture
Home improvements   _____   _____   _____

      Sub total $ $ $

11.   Clothing
New clothes
   Self $ $ $
   Children
Laundry
Dry cleaning
Repairs   _____   _____   _____

      Sub total $ $ $

12.   Transportation
Gas & oil $ $ $
Auto repair & upkeep
Non-commuting bus or train fares   _____   _____   _____

      Sub total $ $ $

13.   Health (not covered by insurance)
Medical $ $ $
Dental
Drugs & medication
Other   _____   _____   _____

      Sub total $ $ $

14.   Personal
Grooming supplies $ $ $
Barber or beauty services
Snacks
Theater & movies
Baby sitter
Hobbies
Vacation

	our past joint expenses	my future expenses	spouse's future expenses
Magazines	$	$	$
Newspapers			
Stationary & postage			
Alcohol			
Tobacco			
Home entertainment			
Other			
Sub total	$	$	$

15. Gifts (beyond the Christmas/Chanukkah funds, above)

	our past joint expenses	my future expenses	spouse's future expenses
Christmas/Chanukkah	$	$	$
Birthdays			
Weddings			
Religious celebrations			
Anniversaries			
Other			
Sub total	$	$	$

16. Contributions

	our past joint expenses	my future expenses	spouse's future expenses
Religious	$	$	$
Charity			
Schools / colleges			
Other			
Sub total	$	$	$
Total flexible expenses	$	$	$
TOTAL EXPENSES	$	$	$

There are _____ additional pages attached to this worksheet

Parental Activity Worksheet

for_____

Enter an M *and* an F for each item to show activity of *both* mother and father
Optional: Estimate time spent per month by each parent on each item

	Past Experience					Future Plans				
	always	usually	equally	seldom	never	always	usually	equally	seldom	never
Change diapers										
Buy clothes										
Cut hair										
Do laundry										
Wash hair										
Make breakfast										
Make lunch										
Make dinner										
Pack lunch, lunch money										
Consult with teachers										
Answer birthday invitations										
Teach to throw ball										
Play										
Read stories										
Buy gifts for parties										
Buy groceries										
Do dishes										
Fill out school papers										
Help with homework										
Arrange for sitters										
Put to bed										
Teach manners										
Teach problem solving										
Make brush teeth										
Arrange birthday parties										
Take trick or treating										
Make bed										
Fold and put away clothes										
Set TV and play rules										
Tend to minor hurts										
Take to doctor for checkup										
Take to dentist										
Tend when sick										
Maintain medical records										
Take to school first day										
Discipline										

	Past Experience					Future Plans				
	always	usually	equally	seldom	never	always	usually	equally	seldom	never
Mend clothes										
Maintain toys										
Teach to clean up										
Pack for trips										
Take to outside lessons										
Take to visit child's friends										
Arrange for friends to come										
Take to Sunday school, church										
Take to sport activities										
Take out to play										
Attend PTA meetings										
Choose best schools, classes										

Others (be specific):

6

What the Legal Divorce is About

The legal divorce has very limited concerns. To get divorced, you have to make decisions about your property, your children, and support. That's it. That's all the legal divorce is about, unless you have a high degree of conflict, in which case it is also about keeping the peace and protecting you, your children and your property.

The law is used to impose a decision only when there is a disagreement that has been brought into court. If you can reach a fair written agreement with your spouse, you can get almost any terms you like without much reference to the laws. Where children are concerned, a judge might take a look at your terms to make sure your children are reasonably well supported and protected.

What you get from your legal divorce is a piece of paper—a Judgment—with findings of fact and court orders on the above subjects. That's all. This is what all the fuss is about; this is what people go to attorneys for and spend tens or hundreds of thousands of dollars to get—a piece of paper with orders about peace, property, custody, and support.

Obviously, these are important subjects, and you need to deal with them anyway. But there are many ways to settle these matters and, in almost all cases, the legal process is very low on the list of recommended methods. You might think that a legal divorce will solve your problems, but it probably won't and it is critically important that you understand this so you don't expect too much from the legal divorce and set yourself up for frustration and disappointment.

Once you understand exactly what the legal divorce is about, you can focus on organizing your facts, negotiation with your spouse and making decisions. As you begin to sort out your new life and your current problems, it is important to know what help you can get from the law and which problems you will have to solve yourself in some other way. Unfortunately, people often get so wrapped up in the legal divorce that they lose sight of their real-life goals and solutions. While a legal divorce is not exactly useless, never forget that your best and most effective solutions involve personal changes and practical, day-to-day actions that take place outside of the context of laws, lawyers and courts.

Your legal divorce is over when you get your Judgment, but your real divorce is not over until you have your self back; when pain, anger, hurt, blame, and guilt are finished; when your ex-spouse no longer has the power to push your buttons; when you are comfortable in the middle of your own life as a single person. This can happen very soon, many years from now, or never, but this is the real goal of your divorce.

After all we have said to show the limitations of the legal divorce, it may seem contradictory that most of this book is devoted to helping you get through it. But the fact is, to get divorced, you have to go through the legal divorce, and you must settle the issues that society cares most about. The purpose of this book is to help you get through the legal divorce without getting caught up in its traps and harmed by a system that works so badly.

How to learn about the law

You will want to know more about the laws of your state and how they apply to the facts of your case. You will especially want to know how clearly it can be predicted what a judge would do if presented with the facts of your case.

In some states, like California, the laws are so detailed and clear that the outcome—what a judge would do if given your facts—is quite predictable in most situations. This is a great help in negotiation, because the spouses can simply refer to the laws and use them as a guide in settling differences. In other states, however, the laws can be so vague, or the judges have so much discretion, that the only predictable thing is that you will have to spend a great deal on lawyers and legal proceedings to find out what some judge will order.

If you are in a state where the outcome for the facts of your case is not predictable, this simply means that the law is not going to be much help in reaching a settlement. It means that if you can't reach a settlement, you will have to spend a lot of time and money getting to court so some stranger (the judge) can make decisions about your property and your children after spending very little time hearing the facts of your life. You should work very hard to settle your case by negotiation and mediation, otherwise, you are in for a long, unpleasant and expensive journey through the legal system.

In addition to matters of substance, you will also want to know practical, procedural things, like where papers are filed, how long it takes to get a judgment, and how much the filing fee is for a divorce case. Things like that.

Here are some ways you can get information about the laws of your state:

The cheapest thing you can do is read a self-help book on the divorce laws of your state. Nolo Press publishes the famous *How to Do Your Own Divorce* books in California and Texas. For other states, go to a book store or library and search the *Books In Print* subject matter catalog under "Divorce," where you will find a section of state-by-state listings. Most states have self-help divorce books; however, the quality ranges from excellent to terrible and it may not be easy to tell the difference. The worst thing would be an old book that has not kept up with changes, leaving you to study laws that no longer exist and working with wrong information, so check the date of printing. Ask the reference librarian or store personnel to make recommendations.

In California, you can call Divorce Helpline, a new kind of law firm that exists only to help people get themselves through divorce. Their attorneys are expert at helping people solve problems and reach settlement. Working by mail, phone, and fax, they offer legal information, advice, help with negotiations and mediation. They will also draft marital settlement agreements and do your paper-work for you. The best thing is that they offer fixed fees for services and they will work with both spouses if you want them to. If you are in California, call 1-800-359-7004. It's the latest and best thing in the divorce field.

You can go see a divorce attorney, but first read about choosing and using a lawyer in Chapter 11. Getting information from a lawyer can be relatively reasonable and efficient if you go prepared and have specific goals in mind. Learn as much as you can ahead of time. It is best to find a lawyer who specializes in divorce—at least 50% of their case load.

We strongly recommend that you get advice from a lawyer trained in divorce mediation who *practices it professionally*. Mediation-minded attorneys are more likely to give you neutral and problem-solving advice, whereas traditional attorneys tend to be more oriented to conflict and their advice tends to be adversarial.

Make sure the attorney understands that you are there for only information and advice and that you are not, at this time, retaining them to handle your case. In fact, it will be best if you never retain an attorney at all, as you will discover in the next chapter.

Before your first visit to an attorney, get yourself prepared by working through Chapter 5. The more informed and clear you are, the faster and cheaper you can get what you need. If you don't know what you want to find out, or if you can't make up your mind about things, wait until your mind clears. Otherwise you may end up paying $150-350 an hour for hand-holding, or you may get talked into legal action you don't need.

Dissolving the bonds

There are three ways to end a marriage:
- divorce (or dissolution),
- legal separation (or separate maintenance), and
- annulment (or nullity).

Separation gets you the same orders for peace, property, custody and support as a divorce, but the parties stay married. Some people have moral or religious reasons for not wanting a divorce, or sometimes there is an economic reason—such as where there are sizable retirement, Social Security or Veteran's benefits to be lost in case of divorce, or where one spouse is a dependent under the other spouse's health insurance program and has a health problem that would cause a hardship if the coverage were lost. An annulment declares that the marriage never existed at all, because the marriage was illegal at the outset or founded on fraud.

You can't stop a divorce. Even if only one spouse wants a divorce and the other resists, there will be a divorce. At best you can slow things down a bit, but the most you will get is a contest on the terms of property, custody or support. One of the major traps in the legal divorce, the thing that leads to a lot of unnecessary expense and unnecessary battles, is that people get so emotionally upset about breaking up that they fight over anything that can be fought over and have contests on the wrong issues for the wrong reasons. But the divorce goes through anyway.

What follows is a check-list of things you will want to clarify when you learn the rules that apply in your state:

Grounds: Almost all states have "no-fault" divorce. In such cases, the court is not concerned at all with who is to blame for the marriage not working out—there's no future in trying to untangle that can of worms—but only with the facts and circumstances of the property, custody and support issues. Some states also have grounds for divorce that involve fault and, unfortunately, a few states permit fault to influence awards of property and support, although this is becoming increasingly rare.

Residency: Most states have a residency requirement that must be satisfied before you can get a divorce: some minimum period of weeks or months that you must have lived in the state just prior to filing your papers or requesting your judgment. Being away temporarily, as on business trips or vacations, is okay and does not count against your residency time. If one spouse is on active military duty, the divorce cannot be filed without that spouse's cooperation or legal motions.

Waiting periods: Some states impose a waiting period or a minimum amount of time that must pass before the divorce can become effective. In a few states, the couple must have been living separately for a stated period of time before the divorce. These delays are supposed to give the couple a last chance to reconcile. It is always possible to get valid orders on the legal issues (peace, property, custody, support) earlier than the divorce date. Legal separation may have no waiting period or a different period from divorce.

Simplified procedures: Many states have procedures that are simplified for some divorces: those by agreement or without objection, or sort-term marriages with no children and minimal property. Many states make it possible to complete a divorce without a court hearing.

Keeping the peace

In cases with high conflict, you may want to go to court for orders to keep the peace or protect yourself, your children or your property. For example, ordering one spouse not to contact, annoy or harass the other; or to move out of the house; or not to encumber or transfer any property except in the usual course of business or for necessities (like paying your divorce attorney); or not to cancel or transfer any insurance held for the benefit of either the other spouse or a child.

If there are children, orders can be made forbidding the removal of a child of the parties from the state without written permission of the other spouse or consent of the court, or for visitation away from the family premises or, if necessary, through a third person.

Restraining orders will often help control a bad situation. They are effective in about 85% of all cases. But you also have to find ways to help yourself. Your own attitude and your determination to change things is actually the most important ingredient in any solution. Self-help includes learning new response patterns, joining a support group, calling on friends, clergy or the police for help, moving away, hiding, taking karate classes, and so on.

Property, income and debts

If your estate is tangled and complex, you might need to see an accountant or get some legal advice to help untangle it. If there is a disagreement between the spouses, don't hesitate to get several opinions. Where the law is not clear, try to settle disagreements according to personal values and understandings. Admit that there is room for a difference of opinion. Weigh the amount involved against the cost of a legal battle; it will almost always cost more to fight than to compromise.

Get organized and make decisions: In order to get through a legal divorce, you have to itemize, characterize, value, and divide all your property. The Assets worksheet in Chapter 5 will help you do this. You will need to develop the following information:
- Itemize: what property do you own?
- Characterize: label each item as to whether it is subject to division (acquired during marriage) or not subject to division (in

most states, this is property acquired before marriage and, possibly, after separation). Learn the rules of property division for your state before you do this step.
- Value: how much is the property to be divided worth?
- Divide: how will it be divided?

Itemize: Make a detailed list of everything of value you own. Small items can be grouped together under a general item heading, such as "jewelry," or "household goods," or "sports equipment."

Characterize: This means labeling each item as whether or not it is subject to division in a divorce. To determine who owns what, you will need to learn more about the laws and how they apply to the facts in your case.

Value: You need to establish the "fair-market value" of property that is to be divided. This does not mean what you paid for an item or what it is worth to you or what it will be worth some day. Fair-market value means what you would get if you sold the property on the open market on the date it is being divided. There is a lot of room for differences of opinion on value, so this is something you would ideally want to work on with your spouse; at least communicate about it so your spouse doesn't think you are trying to be sly. Differences of opinion can be settled by using a professional appraiser. You will need an appraisal anyway for large or hard-to-value items, such as real property, pensions or a going business. You do not have to value property that will be divided exactly in half. For example, if each spouse takes 50 shares of XYZ stock, no one cares how much the shares are worth. If you agree to sell the house (or anything) on the open market and split the net proceeds, the fair value will be determined by the sale.

Divide: Separate (non-marital) property does not get divided because it already belongs to just one person, but it is a very good idea to list and confirm the ownership of valuable or special items for the record and for the sake of clarity in the future. Other property can be divided any way you like by agreement. If you can't agree, it will be divided in court by a judge according to the rules of your state. You will want to learn and understand those rules, but you are especially interested in how predictable they are; that is, can you predict with fair accuracy what a judge would do if presented with the facts of your case? Try very hard to reach agreement through negotiation or mediation, because a legal battle over property will almost always cost more than you can gain by fighting over it. If all else fails, consider binding arbitration; it's cheaper.

Before deciding how to divide any major item of property, it is essential that you understand the tax consequences of changes in title. Read more about this in the section on taxes, below.

The family home and other real estate.
The value of what you own in real estate, or any other property, is called your "equity"—the amount you can actually sell it for on the open market less all amounts owing on it and less the cost of sale. This is the amount that is being divided.

Deciding what to do with a family home is both an emotional and a financial decision. If the home is otherwise a sound investment, owning it can represent security and stability. Or it may be full of memories and ghosts of the past, so it may be bad for you emotionally to stay in it. On the other hand, if you have children, it may be better if they stay in a house, neighborhood and school system they are used to. On the other hand, maybe you can't afford to keep it, or you may need the cash more than security. Or, you could sell the house, move to a more modest accommodation, and invest the money you have saved. Will your decision lock you into your past or will it represent a sound financial investment? Do you need money or stability? You get to decide.

Don't forget to look into tax consequences before you make any decision regarding the family home. A spouse who takes property or money for a share of the home as part of a divorce settlement has no tax liability from that transaction. A spouse who keeps title to the house also keeps the tax basis of the house and future liability for capital gains, if any. If the house is to be sold and proceeds divided later, some time after the divorce, then a spouse who has moved out of the house will (unless it was done very, very carefully) no longer be able to claim the house as a personal residence and may therefore have lost the right to postpone capital gains taxes with a "roll over."

Contact your local IRS office and get a current copy of the free IRS publication number 523, *Tax Information On Selling Your Home.* You will also find valuable information in the Nolo Press tax video mentioned on the inside front cover.

Ten ways to divide property without a fight

This list was originally developed by Judge Robert K. Garth of Riverside, California as an aid to spouses having trouble reaching agreement about the division of their property.

1. **Barter:** Each party takes certain items of property in exchange for other items. For instance, the car and furniture in exchange for the truck and tools.

2. **Choose Items Alternately:** The spouses take turns selecting items from a list of all the marital property, without regard for the value of items selected.

3. **One spouse divides, the other chooses:** One spouse divides all the marital property into two parts and the other spouse gets the choice of parts.

4. **One spouse values, the other chooses:** One spouse places a value on each item of marital property and the other spouse gets the choice of items up to an agreed share of the total value.

5. **Appraisal and alternate selection:** A third person (such as an appraiser) agreed upon by the parties places a value on contested items of marital property and the parties choose alternately until one spouse has chosen items worth his or her share of the marital property.

6. **Sale:** Some or all of the marital property is sold and the proceeds divided.

7. **Secret bids:** The spouses place secret bids on each item of marital property and the one who bids highest for an item gets it. Where one receives items that exceed his or her share of the total value, there will be an equalization payment to the other spouse.

8. **Private auction:** The spouses openly bid against each other on each item of marital property. If one spouse gets more than their share, an equalization payment can be made.

9. **Arbitration:** The spouses select an arbitrator who will decide the matter of valuation and division after hearing from both spouses and considering all evidence.

10. **Mediation:** The spouses select a mediator who works to help them reach an agreement on the matters of valuation and division.

Income and debts.

Learn how income and debts are treated by the laws of your state. Does income after separation belong to both spouses or the one who earns it? Pay attention to retirement benefits or any form of delayed income earned, at least in part, during the marriage.

Learn the rules about who is responsible for debts incurred before, during and after marriage, in one name or both names. It is very important for you to close or remove your name from all joint accounts and credit cards and give *written* notice to creditors that you have dealt with as a couple. Tell them you will no longer be responsible for debts of your spouse. Be sure to tell your spouse before you close accounts or do anything that will effect him or her.

You will always be liable for any debt for which you were liable when it was originally incurred. Orders of the court and agreements between spouses about who must pay particular debts are only effective between the spouses and do not affect the creditor's rights. If your spouse doesn't pay such a debt, *you* are still obligated. This is why many marital settlement agreements have a clause that requires one spouse to notify the other if ever they go bankrupt on debts acquired during the marriage.

Here's a practical scheme for dividing debts that may help you make decisions. It's not based on any law but on the practical idea that debts should go to the person most likely to pay them. If this scheme leads you to an unfair property division, consider an equalization payment—or a note if it can be secured with other property—to make things come out right.

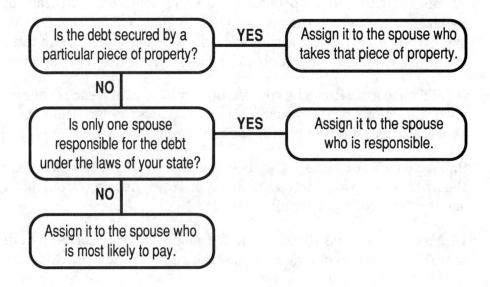

Children: parenting arrangements

If you have children, you will have to create a parenting plan—a detailed schedule and understanding of your arrangements for the future care of your children. This is a difficult issue for divorcing parents, yet it is the most important matter you deal with. It is critically important that you resolve the parenting relationship with a minimum of bad feeling and a maximum of cooperation. Children need both of their parents and the parents need all the help they can get from each other in raising them. Harm to children from divorce is more closely related to conflict *after* the divorce so your goal is to make arrangements that both parents can live with agreeably. See Chapter 10, Protecting Your Children. It is important to try to avoid anything that makes either parent feel he or she is "losing" the child to the other parent. A child is not an object to be won or lost.

Start communicating with your children's other parent to see what will work best for the children and still be comfortable for both of you. To help with the negotiation and planning of child custody matters, use the Parental Activity worksheet in Chapter 5. It will give you a realistic view of how child-rearing chores have been shared in the past and how you intend to share them in the future.

It may help if you learn how your local judges deal with child related issues when parents can't agree. Unfortunately, the rules of law are generally useful only in court, after it's already too late.

Experience shows that pure joint custody—sharing parental rights and responsibility—works best for parents who are cooperative and capable of working out future problems as they come up. The most popular and successful parenting plan provides for joint legal custody for both parents, primary residence (or physical custody) for one parent, and a schedule that shows in great detail exactly when each parent will have custody of the child. This sort of arrangement provides stability while helping reduce the sense of alienation and loss of the out-parent. Finally, there is the old-fashioned award of primary physical *and* legal custody to one parent with a visitation schedule for the other. This is used primarily where the parents are unlikely to be at all cooperative.

A detailed plan helps to create stability, security and to settle any disagreements. After judgment, parents can depart freely from their agreed plan from day-to-day by mutual agreement. But, whenever they can't agree to something different, they can rely on what the plan says. This is why the plan should be as detailed as possible. If the plan is sufficiently detailed, it doesn't matter what terms you use to describe the parenting relationship because the parents will know in any case where the child will be.

Mediation: If you can't agree on a parenting plan, the matter will have to be decided in court—an expensive and destructive process. Before it gets that far, you should try to mediate the issue with the help of a professional mediator. Vast experience shows that a few sessions are usually extremely effective; custody mediation has about an 80% success rate. Some states *require* mediation of custody disagreements. When all else fails, judges often require a home-study by appointed counselors who make recommendations to the court.

After the divorce, if co-parenting does not work well, you should seriously consider professional couples-counseling to help you work better at co-parenting. You can also get a lot of help from the many parent support groups and family service agencies.

Support

Support for children and spouses confronts the inescapable fact that the same old family income now has to support two separate households. Obviously, some changes in life-style are going to be made and the spouse that was least in favor of the divorce will be

most displeased about the "imposed" changes. This is why it is very important to work for mutual acceptance of the divorce and agreement on the terms. Less than half of all support orders are actually paid in full and on time, but support that has been agreed to has a much higher rate of full and timely compliance.

If child or spousal support will be an issue in your case, start by getting all your financial information together by filling out the forms in Chapter 5 and go on to learn the rules of law in your state. Then you can negotiate.

Find out if there are support guidelines in your state and how predictable the amount of support orders is in your local courts. In California, for example, there are statewide mandatory guidelines for child support that judges must follow and most courts have advisory guidelines for spousal support that judges use to assist their thinking. These guides are incorporated in computer programs that are widely used by judges and family law attorneys. If you refer to the guidelines ahead of time, you can fairly accurately predict the level of support that will be awarded in a court contest, so why fight or argue? Just get a computer printout of the guidelines and show it to your spouse. Find out how it works in your state.

Child support orders are always subject to modification, which means that either parent can go back to court at any time to seek a change in the orders. To get a modification, it is generally necessary to show that needs or circumstances have changed since the last order.

Child support takes priority over spousal support. Only after the needs of children are satisfied will the courts consider an award of spousal support. Then the court will try to balance the needs of one spouse against the ability to pay of the other.

The Budget worksheet in Chapter 5 is essential for working on your financial planning. Don't let this slide. Budgeting can be quite tedious and difficult but, especially now, it is *very* necessary. If you have trouble with it, you should seek the help of a financial counselor. To find one, look in the white pages for Consumer Credit Counselors, ask the Better Business Bureau, ask your local bank loan officer, or ask an accountant for references.

Tax issues

There can be important tax consequences to any divorce decision that involves money or property. Pay special attention to:
- your tax filing status;
- how to file returns during the separation period;
- dividing major items of marital property;
- capital gains tax liability, tax basis, and "roll-overs;"
- designating support as child support or family support.

Spouses who can cooperate are definitely in a better position to save money on taxes so you should try to work things out cooperatively for the tax savings, if for no other reason.

Filing status: Your marital status on December 31 determines how you can file your tax returns:

  • If legally married on December 31, you can file as Married Filing Joint or Married Filing Separate, an unfavorable status that is used if you can't get information from your spouse or don't want to share tax liability. You can also file as Head of Household if you have been separated for the last six months of the year and maintain a household for a qualified dependent.

  • If divorced or separated by court order by December 31, you can file as Single, not a favorable status, or you can use the more favorable Head of Household status if you maintain a home for a qualified dependent. This may influence the terms of your parenting arrangement to enable a high-earner to use Head of Household so the parents can share the tax savings.

Dividing major items of property can easily have important tax consequences; this is discussed briefly on page 80. Get advice before dividing a house or any other major capital item.

Child support and Family support: Child support is not included in the income of the recipient and cannot be deducted from the income of the payor. Spousal support is included in the income of the recipient and deducted from the income of the payor. You can agree to pay all or part of child support as "Family Support" which is treated like spousal support. This means the high earner can save on taxes by deducting the payments from income, and the savings can be shared by the couple. Get advice before drafting such an agreement because it won't work if it is not done just right.

Your local IRS office has very useful free booklets. Be *sure* to get IRS publication 504, *Tax Information for Divorced or Separated Individuals* which is full of valuable information. Also consider numbers 503, *Tax Information On Selling Your Home*, and 523, *Child and Dependent Care Expenses*. Depending on how much money and property you have, you may find it worth the cost to consult a tax expert before making decisions and especially before entering into a marital settlement agreement.

7

How to Beat the System

Anatomy of a divorce

Let's take a look now at how a divorce case works so you can see what you have to go through and how you can beat the legal system. The legal divorce process is similar in all states, but the terms will differ. In this book, we will use the first set of terms.

- Spouse who starts the divorce = Petitioner or Plaintiff
- Document filed = Petition or Complaint
- The other spouse = Respondent or Defendant
- Document filed (if any) = Response or Answer
- Orders for divorce and terms = Judgment or Decree

Take a look at the diagram on page 89. All divorces start with a Petition and end with a Judgment. The Petition sets out in very general terms what the facts and issues are and what the Petitioner wants. After being filed with the court, it is served on the other spouse to give notice that the case has started. This is a simple document; filing and serving it is not complicated.

After Petitioner files papers, the other spouse can file a Response if he or she wants to be involved in the legal divorce process. This has to be done within a stated time, usually 30 or 60 days after the Petition is served. The Response is similar to the Petition, a simple document that is easy to do. The effect of the Response is simply to get the other spouse into the case on an equal footing with the Petitioner.

If a Response is filed, the case is "contested." If there is no Response, it is assumed that the Respondent concedes all issues according to the broad terms of the Petition and the case is "uncontested." If the couple has made a written marital settlement agreement before the Petition is filed, there won't be any reason for the second spouse to enter the case.

Contested and uncontested divorces are dramatically different:
- **The uncontested divorce** is simple: it goes straight through paperwork and red-tape to judgment. Some couples will need to work out a written marital settlement agreement beforehand. A routine appearance in court by Petitioner may be required, but

87

many states have simplified procedures that don't require a hearing—uncontested cases are so routine that they don't want to take up valuable court time with them. That's all there is to it. Almost anyone can do their own uncontested divorce (see Chapter 9).

• **Contested divorces** are another matter entirely. Take a minute now to study the diagram on the next page. There are lots of steps in a contested case and each step is quite complex, worth a chapter or a book of its own. This is lawyer country; you can't go through a contested divorce very effectively without one. It takes lots of time, money and emotional suffering to get through a contested divorce.

Any contested case can become uncontested if one spouse simply drops out of the contest or if the spouses reach an agreement—the earlier, the cheaper. However, when you are represented by attorneys, it is much more difficult to reach agreement. When negotiations are conducted through attorneys, it is *extremely* common for a case to drag on and on and run up huge attorneys fees before it settles.

As you can see in the diagram, there are only three ways you can go through the legal system from Petition to Judgment:
• You go with an attorney through the legal system to trial where a Judge will impose decisions about property, children and support;
• More commonly, you go through the legal system until your attorney can negotiate an agreement with your spouse's attorney about property, children and support. Once you have an agreement, all that's left is a lot of paperwork and red-tape.
• You do it yourself. This means that you work out an agreement outside the legal system with no more than limited assistance from attorneys. An agreed, uncontested divorce is so easy that you might as well do it yourself. In fact, as you will see below, doing it yourself has so many advantages that it is the best way of all.

Advantages to a legal contest: It might seem odd after all we've said, but there are *some* advantages to a contested divorce in *some* cases:
• In high conflict cases, you can get some restraining orders;
• If your spouse is playing hardball, it may be better to fight rather than give in;
• Fighting is an outlet for or diversion from the pain of divorce.
• Anger and fighting help sever bonds of attachment and affection.
• There is a chance in some states for material gain—*if* you win.
• And, finally, some people just feel like fighting.

If you have to fight, Chapter 10 discusses how to run a controlled battle effectively and how to avoid some of the worst disadvantages.

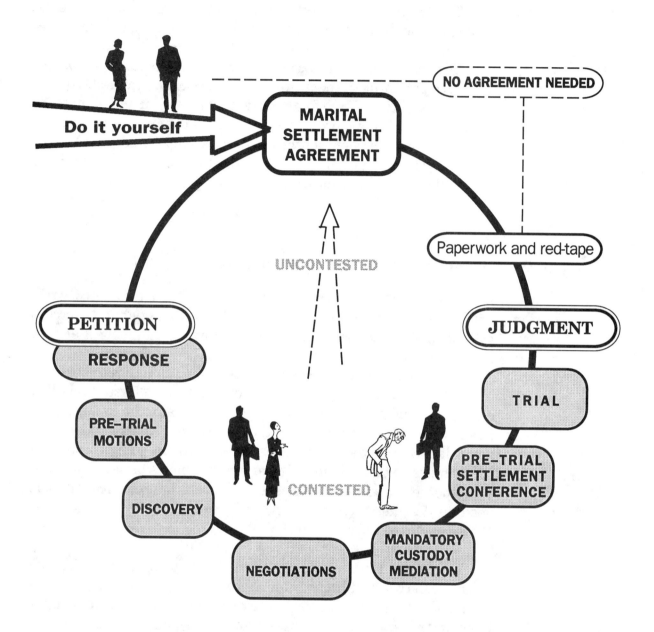

Pretrial motions: Formal motions and hearings to get temporary orders on such things as support, custody, visitation, possession of family home, keep-away, non-molest, freeze assets, prevent sale or waste of assets.

Discovery: A variety of legal tools to dig for information about assets or other issues. Depositions (taking of statements under oath), interrogatories (sworn answers in writing to questions), and demands for copies of documents.

Negotiations: Spouse's lawyers seek written agreements on as many facts and issues as possible. Not a formal part of the system.

Mandatory mediation: Some states require mediation if parties can't agree on child custody and parenting arrangements. If that doesn't work, the judge may require a home study and report by a court-appointed counselor.

Pre-trial settlement conference: An informal meeting with lawyers, clients and a judge who will give an opinion on likely rulings and try to pressure (persuade) parties to settle without trial.

Marital settlement agreement: A written contract to settle all issues. Strongly recommended in any case with significant property, debts or minor children.

The *disadvantages* to a legal contest, however, are *very* impressive:
- Both sides get drained financially and emotionally.
- Two lawyers double the personalities in the case and increase the distance and complexity of every communication, making settlement much more difficult.
- Kids can get harmed, perhaps permanently; chances for cooperative co-parenting in the future will be seriously impaired.
- Imposed terms are often not adhered to, so you end up in more hassles, spending more money and time on enforcement.
- Your upset becomes entrenched, runs deeper and lasts longer. Since your real goal is to get on with your life, this holds you back and down—perhaps forever.

How the legal system works against you

If there were no legal system, no lawyers and no courts, divorce would still be difficult and it would still take time to go through it. Divorce is at least a major crossroad in your life, maybe even a full-blown life crisis.

So, here you are, you and your spouse, going through your personal life changes, when the State comes along and says, "Excuse me! You can't go through this without us. Your divorce has to be conducted on *our* field and under *our* rules ...and you can't even *hope* to understand our rules. By the way, this divorce system we're going to put you through has *no* tools for helping you solve problems or negotiate with your spouse. In fact, our legal system is based on conflict and it is specially designed to cause trouble and greatly increase your expense. Please pay your filing fees on the way in."

Our system of justice is known as an "adversary system." This is the nature of the beast. It began hundreds of years ago in the middle ages with "trial by combat," where people with a disagreement would fight it out and whoever survived was "right." Today, physical contact is no longer a recognized legal technique, but things are still set up as a fight. The parties are regarded as adversaries, enemies in combat. When a divorce is conducted in our legal system, the spouses and their attorneys are expected to struggle against one another and try to "win" the case, to "beat" the opposition. The rules control the way your attorney works with you. Your attorney is *required* to be "adversarial," that is, aggressive and combative. The adversary system and the way lawyers work in it is a major cause of conflict, trouble and the high cost of divorce. You want to have as little as possible to do with the legal system.

In spite of the way things seem, lawyers are not always villains and not always to blame for stirring up conflict. Conflict is already lively in most divorces; in fact, lawyers are often more moderate than their clients. But even for lawyers who mean well, the tools they use and the system they work in will usually increase conflict. Law schools have no course requirements in counseling, family dynamics, or communication skills, and very little or nothing on negotiation. Legal training stresses manipulation of rules of law, aggressive and defensive strategy, how to take any side of any case and make the most of it, how to argue, and how to get the most financial advantage in every situation.

Professional standards of practice dictate how a lawyer will conduct your case. For example, professional ethics forbid your lawyer to communicate directly with your spouse—the adversary. It is expected, instead, that your spouse will be represented by an attorney and your lawyer can only communicate through your spouse's lawyer. Your attorney can't "talk sense" to your spouse, or explain to your spouse how you see things, or even help you talk to each other. It means your attorney will *always* have a one-sided view of your case and can never achieve an understanding any greater than your own.

Here's what your attorney *can* do. In the diagram on page 89, the lower portion shows all the steps in a contested divorce. These are the retained attorney's tools—the only tools the law has to offer. Apart from advice, any help you get from a retained attorney will come from these tools or in the form of a letter threatening to use one of these tools.

If you retain a lawyer, he will definitely take your case into the contested cycle of the legal system because that's the only thing he can do. He has to. There are no other formal tools.

The primary tools the lawyer uses are pre-trial motions and discovery. An attorney can take you and your spouse into court to get temporary orders for support, custody, visitation or keeping the peace. An attorney can use formal discovery to get documents and information under oath. If you and your spouse can work out your own temporary arrangements and share all information openly, you'll have no need for those incredibly expensive legal tools. You can keep your case out of lawyers' offices and out of court.

If either spouse is represented by an attorney, that attorney will invariably write letters, file legal papers, make motions, and do discovery. These actions will compel the other spouse to get an attorney, too. Then, the case will become contested and the cost and conflict level will go up. In negotiations, attorneys tend to ask for more than they expect to get; it's considered "good" practice. Your spouse's lawyer will oppose your lawyer's exaggerated demands by offering less than they are willing to give and by attacking you and your case at the weakest points. Now you're off to a good, hot start and soon you'll have a hotly contested case, lots of cost, and a couple of very upset spouses. Fees in contested cases can run from tens of thousands of dollars *each* all the way up to *everything*.

Summary: Except in high-conflict cases, the legal system has little to offer. The things an attorney can do for you are expensive, upsetting, and tend to increase conflict rather than reduce it. If you don't want to (or have to) use the legal system, go around it—work out your arrangements outside the legal system and, if necessary, get limited assistance, in the form of information and advice, from attorneys who do not represent the spouses.

How to beat the system

Of course you want to get your Judgment—that's your legal divorce—but you don't want to go through the adversarial legal system to get it; you don't want to get tangled up with lawyers and courts. So, you don't go *through* the legal system, you go *around* it. You work outside the legal system to make arrangements and reach an agreement with your spouse. Look again at page 89.

Doing things yourself, you have far more control and far better solutions. Working outside the legal system is the way you get a low conflict, low impact, higher quality divorce.

To stay outside the legal system, you do not *retain* an attorney. *Neither* spouse should retain one. The key word is "retain." If you follow the methods in this book, you may not need any help at all from an attorney. But I'm not saying you shouldn't get help from an attorney if you want it, just that you should not *retain* an attorney unless you have no other choice.

Retaining an attorney means the attorney takes professional responsibility for, and control of, your case. The attorney represents you. You sign a retainer agreement, then you pay $1,000 to $5,000 dollars "on retainer" and your attorney has now taken over control of your case. This is what they mean when they say, "I'll take your case." And they do take your case—right into high-conflict, low solution legal system. They have to; it's the law.

Because you don't want to go into a system that works so hard against you, you must not retain an attorney unless you have no other choice. You need to retain an attorney if you are facing immediate threat of harm. You need an attorney if you:
- have some reason to believe that your spouse poses a danger to you, your children or your property;
- can't get support from your spouse and have no way to live;
- think your spouse is transferring, selling or hiding assets.

In such cases, you should get a good attorney right away; otherwise, you don't want one, except for information and advice. The attorney retainer is the poison apple—don't bite it.

If you feel uneasy about not retaining an attorney, don't worry; in the rest of this book, you are going to learn very effective things you can do for yourself and how to get help if you need it.

There are three different kinds of cases that respond to self-help techniques:
- no agreement between the spouse is needed;
- an agreement will be fairly easy to work out;
- an agreement is needed but it may not be easy to work it out.

No agreement needed or spouse not involved. In some cases, an agreement between the spouses either isn't necessary or not possible. In some cases, this is because there are no children, very little property, few debts to worry about, no need for support—in short, nothing to agree to. There are also cases where the Respondent simply will not participate and will not file a Response. Respondent is either long gone or simply doesn't care. In such cases, there's no way to negotiate and nothing for Petitioner to do but go through some paperwork and red-tape. If you have this kind of case, go to Chapter 9 where you'll learn how to get your divorce.

Agreement needed. Most couples, however, *do* need an agreement or *should* have one. If you have children, you should work out a good parenting plan in a written agreement. If you have income or property worth protecting, or lots of debts to be paid, or if you need to work out spousal or child support arrangements, you should definitely have a written agreement. If Respondent is involved and cares how the divorce is going to be arranged, you should have an agreement. The question now is how difficult it will be for you to work out the terms of your agreement and whether or not you will need help to do it.

Agreement will be easy to work out. If you think it will be no problem for you and your spouse to work out an agreement, you can go straight to Chapter 9 and read about what to do next. The rest of this chapter is about the advantages of agreement and Chapter 8 is about how to overcome the obstacles to agreement and how to negotiate with your spouse.

Agreement may not come easily. This describes the situation for most couples going through divorce. If both spouses are involved and concerned, and if you want to learn how to work out an agreement without retaining an attorney, keep reading. You will find out that things you can do to help yourself are far more effective than anything a lawyer can do for you. You will learn about the obstacles to agreement and how to overcome them, how to negotiate effectively with your spouse, and where to get help if you have trouble with the negotiations.

Advantages of an agreement

We've already seen that the marital settlement agreement (MSA) is your key to avoiding lawyers and the legal system, but that's not all. It has many other important advantages. Your MSA actually becomes your Judgment; it is either attached and incorporated in the Judgment or the Judgment will be written to include all the terms of your agreement. You get the same result either way. Once you sign your MSA, your divorce is essentially over. All that's left is red tape and paperwork.

With a good MSA you get total control over your Judgment because you decide all the terms ahead of time. Without an agreement, you can't be sure exactly what some judge might do. The MSA has far more depth, detail, flexibility and protection than a plain Judgment. Almost anything that's on your mind or in your lives can be included and resolved any way you like.

Some states have simplified procedures that allow you to get your divorce without going to court—if you have an agreement. Without an agreement, you almost certainly will have to go to a hearing to get your Judgment.

What's most important is that you get a better divorce outcome when you work out an agreement. This means that after the Judgment, it's far more likely that support will be paid in full and on time, parenting agreements will go smoothly and cooperatively, and you'll have better post-divorce relationships. With an agreement, people tend to heal faster and it just plain feels better.

The agreement you are about to negotiate is very valuable and worth working very hard to get.

The main message

To beat the legal system you don't go through it, you go around it. You don't take the low road, you take the high road. These are your keys to the highway:
   • You and your spouse work out an agreement
   • outside the legal system
   • without either spouse retaining an attorney.
You can get advice from attorneys, you can get an attorney/ mediator to help you work out your agreement, but you do not retain an attorney to handle your divorce. Once you have an agreement, you have an uncontested case and there's nothing left to do but red-tape and paperwork. If you don't need an agreement, so much the better: just do the paperwork and you're done.

8

HOW TO GET AN AGREEMENT:
—dealing with disagreement and conflict

This chapter is about how to deal with divorce in cases where the spouses are in active disagreement, including the whole range from simple difference of opinion to active upset and anger. As you will see, the things you can do yourself are far more effective than anything a lawyer can do for you. The next chapter is about what to do after you reach an agreement, and Chapter 10 is about dealing with extreme conflict and what to do if you don't want to or can't agree. We are addressing a very wide range of possible situations here, so just use whatever seems useful for your own situation.

Over 90% of all cases are settled before they get to trial, so *your* case is *very* likely to settle. Unfortunately, too many are settled only after the spouses have spent their emotional energies on conflict and their financial resources on lawyers. The time and effort spent battling has impaired their ability to get on with their lives and may have caused serious psychic damage to themselves and their children. The spouses could have saved themselves all that simply by agreeing to settle earlier. Why didn't they?

The five obstacles to agreement

Okay, here you are, heading for a divorce; your spouse is going to be involved and you want to work out an agreement. What's so hard about that? Why don't you just get together and do it? Easier to say than to do, isn't it? There are good reasons why it's hard for spouses to work out an agreement—five, to be exact:
- emotional upset and conflict;
- insecurity and fear;
- ignorance and misinformation;
- the legal system and lawyers; and, finally,
- real disagreement.

To get an agreement, in or out of the system, with or without an attorney, you have to overcome the five obstacles. Let's look at them in a little more detail to see what you're dealing with:

1. Emotional upset and conflict: This is about high levels of anger, hurt, blame, and guilt— a very normal part of divorce. If one or both spouses are upset, you can't negotiate, have reasonable discussions or make sound decisions. Complex and volatile emotions become externalized—attached to things or to the children. When emotions are high, reason is at its lowest ebb and will not be very effective *at that time*. There are various causes of upset:
  • the divorce itself, stress of major change, broken dreams, fear of change, fear of an unknown future;
  • different degrees of acceptance of the idea of divorce and willingness to proceed—sometimes the biggest obstacle of all;
  • history of bad communication habits or conflict;
  • particular events or circumstances (a new lover, a new debt).

2. Insecurity, fear, lack of confidence, unequal bargaining power: You can't negotiate if either spouse feels incompetent, afraid, or that the other spouse has some big advantage. Divorce is tremendously undermining and tends to multiply any general lack of self-confidence and self-esteem. Also, there are often very real causes for insecurity: lack of skill and experience at dealing with business and negotiation, and lack of complete information and knowledge about the process and the marital affairs. It doesn't matter if insecurity is real or reasonable; it *is* real if it *feels* real.

3. Ignorance and misinformation: Ignorance about the legal system and how it works can make you feel uncertain, insecure and incompetent. You feel as if you don't know what you are doing ...and you are right. Misinformation is when the things you think you know are not correct. Misinformation comes from friends, television, movies, even from lawyers who are not family law specialists. It can distort your expectations about your rights and what's fair. It's hard to negotiate with someone who has mistaken ideas about what the rules are. Fortunately, both conditions can be easily fixed with *reliable* information.

4. The legal system and lawyers: We've discussed this at length. It does not help you overcome obstacles to agreement but, rather it is one of the major obstacles that you have to overcome. You want to avoid the legal system as much as possible—and you can.

5. Real disagreement: These are the real issues that you want to deal with rationally and negotiate with your spouse. Real disagreement is based on the fact that the spouses now have different needs and interests. After dealing with the first four

obstacles, these real issues may turn out to be minor, but even if they are serious, at least they can be negotiated rationally.

The solutions are in your hands. Apart from the legal system—which you can avoid—all obstacles to your agreement are personal, between you and your spouse and between you and yourself. The solutions to your problems are entirely in your own hands and the legal system has little to offer compared with the potential for harm, and especially compared with all the things you can do for yourself outside the legal system.

Take care. Pay special attention to emotional upset and especially insecurity and fear. These are the forces that drive people into a lawyer's office. You want to avoid doing anything that might increase the upset and fear of either spouse.
- The upset person is saying, "I can't stand this, I won't take it anymore! I'm going to get a lawyer!"
- The insecure person is saying, "I can't understand all this, I can't deal with it, I can't deal with my spouse. I want to be safe. I need someone to help me. I'm going to get a lawyer."

And this is how cases get dragged into unnecessary legal conflict.

You need to arrange things so both spouses are comfortable about not retaining an attorney. If you think your spouse may be upset or insecure, you have to be very careful and patient. If *you* are feeling incapable of dealing with your own divorce, the information in this book will help a lot and you will see that you can get all the help and support you need without *retaining* an attorney.

How to overcome the obstacles to agreement

You're going to be working on your agreement outside the legal system, because the things you can do to help yourself outside the legal system are far more effective than anything a lawyer can do for you. But you don't just walk up to your spouse and start negotiating. The first step is to get ready and get prepared; you have to do something about the obstacles to disagreement. You have to calm emotional upset, reduce fears, and balance the bargaining power of both parties, get correct information and advice, and know how to get safe, reliable help if you need it. Then you can get down to negotiating your real issues.

Here are ten specific things you can do to help yourself. These steps will help you deal with the obstacles so you can get to negotiation.

1. Make some "New Life" Resolutions: Start thinking of yourself as a whole and separate person. You may feel wounded, but you are healing and becoming whole and complete. Keep that picture in mind. Pain and confusion is part of healing. Let go of old attachments, old dreams, old patterns that don't work; this is your chance to build new ones. Decide you will not be a victim of your spouse or the system or yourself. You will not try to change or control your spouse—that's all over now, it doesn't work, it's contrary to meaning of divorce. Concentrate on yourself, especially on your own actions. You can do something about what your spouse does by changing what you do. Take responsibility for yourself: if anyone hurts or upsets you, try to understand how you let them do that. Remember the old saying, "If your dog bites me once, shame on him; if he bites me twice, shame on me." Concentrate on your physical health, your work, children, friends. Try to become quiet and calm. Keep your life as simple as possible.

2. Insulate and protect your children: Involving children is going to upset the spouses and harm your children. Keep them well away from the divorce. Tell them the truth in simple terms they can understand, but otherwise, don't discuss the divorce in front of them. Don't involve the children or pass messages through them. Don't let them hear your arguments or hear you criticize their other parent. Let them know you both love them and will always be their mother and father, no matter what happens between you. Help them understand that loving their other parent is not a betrayal of you; they shouldn't have to choose sides. Help them establish a new pattern of stability so they feel safe and help them have as much contact as possible with both parents.

3. Get safe, stable and secure, just for a while: Your first and most important job is to do *whatever* you have to do to arrange short-term safety, stability, and security for yourself, the children, and your spouse—in that order. This doesn't mean forever, just for a month or a few months at a time. Don't be concerned yet about the long-term or the final outcome, and we're talking about minimum conditions here, not your old standard of living. Don't even try to do anything else until minimum conditions are met. You can't negotiate if you don't know where you will live or how you will eat, or if you are afraid for your safety or if you think your house is about to be foreclosed or your car repossessed. You can't negotiate if your spouse is not in a safe and stable situation, too.

If you can't get both spouses stabilized, the fear and the upset level will go up and you will probably end up in court with attorneys arguing over pre-trial motions. Your case will get dragged into the legal system, fighting in court at a very early stage. These legal procedures are tremendously upsetting and *very* expensive, on the order of tens of thousands of dollars for each side. To avoid this kind of outcome, you have to help each other even if you don't feel like it.

4. Agree on temporary arrangements: If you can work out your own temporary arrangements, you won't need an attorney to get you temporary court orders. Start by agreeing that you want a fair result and will both act fairly. Agree to communicate before doing anything that will affect the other spouse or the estate or the children. The goal here is to avoid surprises and upset and includes things like closing accounts or starting legal actions.

It takes a long time for things to settle down and for the spouses to work out a final agreement. Meanwhile, you have to arrange for the support of two households on the same old income, the parenting of minor children, making payments on mortgages and debts, and so on. Preferably, this should be done in writing. If you have trouble, use techniques and resources discussed below.

5. Slow down, take some time: If you can make your situation safe and stable for a while, you don't have to be in a hurry. Think of divorce as an illness or an accident; it really is a kind of injury, and it takes time to heal. You have to go slow and easy, be good to yourself. Some very important work goes on during this slowdown. You work on reducing emotional upset—this takes time; you work on mutual acceptance—this takes time; you work to help both spouses become confident, stable, secure. This is a good time to get reliable information and advice, find out what the rules are.

6. Get information and advice: First, organize your facts, records and documents (Chapter 5). You'll want lists of assets, deeds, statements, account numbers, income and expense information, tax returns and wage stubs. Get information from your records and from your accountant, from recent tax returns, and from your spouse. Spouses should have a full and open exchange of information: it helps to build trust and confidence, and, in many states, it's the law, so you might as well just go ahead and do it. If information is not exchanged freely outside of the legal system, you will probably end up in court with attorneys doing very expensive discovery work.

You should learn the rules for divorce in your state as they apply to your case. You especially want to know how predictable the outcome would be if your facts were taken before a judge. You may find some useful books on the laws of divorce for your state (see Chapter 6) or you may decide to get some legal advice. Make sure your spouse has a copy of this book, then maybe you can discuss some of the issues and ideas in it. At least you will both be aware of what a divorce is about and the consequences of combat.

Be very careful where you get advice. Your friends and relatives will be a fountain of free advice, *but don't take it*—the price is too high if they're wrong. They mean well, but probably don't know what they're talking about. You *should* use your friends for emotional support but take advice only from an attorney who specializes in divorce. Don't take advice from paralegals or people who run typing services; they're not trained for it. In California, you can call Divorce Helpline and consult their attorneys.

7. Focus on needs and interests; don't take positions yet: A position is a stand on a final outcome: "I want the house sold and the children every weekend." In the beginning, there's too much upset and too little information to decide what you want for an outcome and, besides, positions are a set up for an argument: the other side either agrees or disagrees. It's better to think and talk in terms of needs and interests. These are more basic concerns: "I want what's fair and what the rules say is mine; I need to be secure and have enough to live on; I want to know what I can count on for living expenses; I want maximum contact with my children; I need to get out of debt, especially on the credit cards; I want an end to argument and upset." Put this way, these are goals that you and your spouse can discuss together.

8. Stick with short-term solutions: Concentrate on short-term solutions to immediate problems like keeping two separate households afloat for a few months; keeping mortgages paid and cars from being repossessed; keeping children protected, secure, stable, in contact with both parents. These are things you can possibly work on together.

9. Minimum legal activity: You want to avoid any legal activity unless it is necessary—zero is best, or the minimum required to protect yourself or get your case started. Ideally, you will avoid retaining an attorney and you won't give your spouse any reason to retain an attorney.

10. Get help if you need it: For yourself or your children, consider counseling or therapy. For help with talking to your spouse, consider couples counseling or go see a mediator. These low-conflict professionals can help with emotional issues, defusing upset or, in the case of the mediator, with making temporary arrangements.

How to reduce conflict

Reducing conflict *never* means for you to compromise your rights or self-respect, but it *is* hard work. Struggling with it can help *you* a great deal even if it doesn't actually reach your spouse or get you an agreement. Those are by–products. The real benefit is inside.

Conflict is what happens when two people have a different way of looking at the same facts or have to reconcile different goals and interests. It happens all the time; so what? *Healthy* conflict leads to solutions. It's not always easy, but you can usually work things out through discussion and compromise. *Unhealthy* conflict is when negative emotions pervert or displace an otherwise honest disagreement. The emotions that fuel unhealthy conflict are a combination of each spouse's own ancient attitudes, experiences, and habits coupled with all the patterns and distortions built up in the relationship. Untangling any part of this terrible can of worms will be a blessing for the rest of your life.

If you are like most couples—and not just divorcers—you have a predictable pattern of interaction that doesn't work. You have your own personal set of triggers that will set you off more or less the same way every time, over and over again. You have habit patterns for dealing with disagreement that do not serve you well or solve any problems. It may not be intentional, it may not even be conscious, but you know each other's buttons and you both push them automatically, without even thinking, especially when feeling angry, frightened or guilty.

Don't do that anymore.

Maybe it doesn't take much of a push on a button to get your bell to ring; maybe you are so upset that it rings almost by itself. Maybe your spouse is in a highly emotional condition too, acting like someone you wish you never knew, and you are taking it all very personally. Don't do that either.

Stop letting your mate's moods dominate your life. That's over. You don't need to do it any longer. That's what divorce is for—you are not divorcing just your spouse, you are also divorcing yourself from all those old patterns that didn't work and won't work. The divorce starts to work for you when you learn to untangle yourself from all those ugly dances you used to do. If you just stop (not easy to do), your mate may keep on, but will eventually have to notice that it's a solo performance. If not, too bad, but your ex-mate's problems aren't yours. *Your* problem is how *you* act, how *you* feel, and how to handle your own life.

You probably can't control your mate, nor should you try to, but you have a better chance if you concentrate on healing your own emotions and controlling your own actions. That's your whole focus now. We are talking about controlling *actions* here, not feelings. Don't try to control your feelings, they are real and valid. Observe your feelings, accept them, but express them some other way.
Stop. Breathe. Don't react.
Pay attention to what's going on for you. Are you angry? Hurt? Afraid? ....What? Be curious; investigate yourself and the scene.
Stop. Breathe. Don't react. Say that over and over quietly to yourself whenever things start to pop loose.

Curiosity is a great attitude and a great tool. Even while an event is in progress, you can be trying to figure out what the anger is all about. Anger is the flip-side of fear. When someone is afraid, the least little thing will set them off into a crisis of reactive anger. Fear is mostly unconscious and usually about not having enough— not enough security, power, respect, love or stability. Fear is about loss of face, not being in control, not having enough money, fear of change, fear of responsibility, things like that. What is your spouse afraid of? What are *you* afraid of?

To figure out what anger is about, you have to listen. Honest, open listening is the best thing you can do when someone is angry. You don't have to buy into their anger or agree with their point-of-view, just understand. If you are sincerely trying to hear what the angry person is saying and understand what's *behind* the anger— if you are not reacting to it, defending yourself from it, arguing, denying, dismissing or patronizing—then their anger will have nothing to feed on and will spend itself sooner. The angry person may save face by staying huffy and self-righteous, but your attitude will be noticed and will have a cumulative effect over time. If not fed, anger collapses from its own weight.

The most constructive thing you can do—and this is a difficult ideal—is to try to figure out the mutual patterns that never did and still don't work. More particularly, you want to understand the part you play. Don't try to change anything, not at first; just observe when it's happening. Stop. Breathe. Even if you don't untangle the web, taking this attitude will be a big improvement. Whenever you catch it happening, just observe, don't respond. Notice how easily you fall into the old routine, how bad you feel after. Ooops, did it again. It's hard to stop, like asking a trout not to flash at splashing flies; like quitting an addiction cold turkey, only harder because you probably aren't always aware when you are doing it. Breaking old bad habits will greatly increase your future happiness. You may be able to do it by yourself, but some good professional help could be very useful at this point.

Working on your self is the most interesting of all possible paths. It may be the hardest—and most rewarding—thing you will ever do. This is when you develop your sense of personal responsibility. You are breaking your psychological dependency on your spouse, no longer depending on your mate for your own sense of well-being and worth; you will no longer let your feelings be determined by your mate's moods and actions. You and *only* you are responsible for your feelings and your actions. It isn't your fault when you are down, or anyone else's, but it *is* your responsibility to get up.

When times are hard, pay special attention to your body. Take care of it; relax it; be good to it. This is a healing time. Eat well, get healthy. Slow down, be quiet, hole-up, nest. Get massage, work on those knots. Take hot baths and/or cold showers, whatever works. Feeling bad isn't so bad if you don't feel bad about it. Just let it happen; it's proof you're alive and learning.

You know how sometimes it's easy for you to see what's *really* going on between two arguing people? Or how you can observe other people's patterns when they can't? What if someone could do that for you now? This is a good time to get some third person to listen, observe, give you feedback and advice. That's what professional family counselors are trained to do. Counseling and how to choose a counselor are discussed below.

Friends are wonderful moral support, but don't take advice from just anybody. Listen only to people who have wisdom and experience. Being a friend and caring about you doesn't make that person qualified to give good advice. If your friend is helping you get worked up, dwell on grievances or wallow in your stuff, get your advice somewhere else.

Practical Pointers:

1. Anger is not reasonable. When someone reaches the flash point, the ability to reason gets less as anger increases. Don't bother trying to talk sense until the anger is well past. Anger always passes. It runs its course faster if you don't feed it, faster yet if you use de-fusing techniques (below).

2. Deal with the problem, not the person.

3. You do not have to give in or be a doormat. **Rights:** You have the right to act in your own best interest; to respect and stand up for yourself; to politely express ideas and honest emotions; to ask for what you want; to set limits; to be treated with respect and dignity; to make mistakes and accept responsibility. **Responsibilities:** It is your responsibility to respect and honor the same rights for your mate; to take responsibility for your own behavior.

4. How to be assertive *and* constructive: **Confront** the problem, not the person. **De-fuse** the hostility, don't play at patterns that don't work. Your goal is to keep things calm so you can deal with the problem or complete the business at hand. **Disengage** from the conflict. Pay attention to your own anger level; when necessary, express your need to interrupt the cycle and allow a cool-down period. Re-schedule another time to work on the problem, then get up and quietly leave.

5. De-fusing: Here are some basic techniques for de-fusing anger when you run into it:
   • First, remain calm yourself. Don't react. Instead, use your sense of curiosity; become an interested observer. Encourage talking by listening openly.
   • *Show* that you understand or are trying to. Nod, paraphrase and mirror what you hear ("Let's see if I have this right; you are saying that ......"). You must be sincere in this for it to work well.

106

• Talk to your spouse with "I" messages instead of the accusing "you." For example, "I can't discuss this when the TV is on so loud," instead of "You are noisy and totally inconsiderate."

• Make statements about yourself when necessary, but *not* about your mate personally. Be specific and concrete, be positive not negative.

• Set your limits ("If you keep yelling, I am going to leave," or "If you are more than 30 minutes late picking up the children, I will have to leave with them.").

• Don't defend or attack, don't generalize ("You always do this to me"), don't be sarcastic or discuss your mate's motives or dig up old history.

• Deal with the specific matter now at hand.

• Reassure your mate; help him or her to save face.

• Remember, your goal is to reach agreement, not score points.

6. Work with the attitude that you want to find solutions that allow you *both* to get what you want and need. Avoid the win/lose attitude.

7. Don't expect a quick-fix or miracles. You can do all the right things and not have immediate results. It's like erosion, the sort of thing you have to chip away at. It takes time, but you *will* succeed if you keep at it.

There is a lot of popular material on dealing with anger and conflict, how to be assertive in a constructive way, and some good material on how to talk and listen to your family. It can only help if you read some of it. Take a look at the reading list in the back.

How to negotiate with your spouse

The best predictor of a good divorce outcome is *client* rather than attorney control of negotiation. This doesn't mean you should not get help and advice from an attorney when you want it, it means you are better off if you plan to do most or all of the negotiating yourself. This is also realistic because studies indicate that clients feel their attorneys don't actually give them much help or guidance anyway.

In a 1976 Connecticut study, nearly half of those interviewed reported no more than three contacts with their attorney, *including* phone calls, while 60% said they had worked out all issues without attorney help. In a New Jersey study in 1984, which considered only cases with children where *both* spouses had attorneys, less than 20% felt their lawyers had played a major role in settlement negotiations. So, you are likely to end up dealing with the negotiation anyway, and there is strong evidence that you are far better off if you do. You get a higher degree of compliance with terms of agreement, a much lower chance for future courtroom conflict, and a lot more general good will. This is especially important if you have children and co-parenting to consider.

Don't expect negotiating with a spouse to be easy. There are lots of built-in difficulties—so many that you may want professional help from a good mediator. But, okay, so there are problems—what to do? Here are ten steps you can take to make negotiation work:

1. Be business-like: We discussed this at length in Chapter 4.
• Keep business and personal matters separate. You can talk about personal matters any time, but *never* discuss business without an appointment and an agenda. This is so you can both be prepared and composed.
• Act business-like: be on time and dress for business. Don't socialize and don't drink; it impairs your judgment.
• Be polite and insist on reasonable manners in return. If things start to sneak into the personal or become un-business-like, say you're going to stop if the meeting doesn't get back on track. Ask to set another date. If matters don't improve, don't argue, don't get mad, just get up and go.

2. Meet on neutral ground: Find a neutral place to meet, not the home or office of either spouse where there could be too many reminders, memories, personal triggers. Or the visiting spouse could feel at some disadvantage and the home spouse can't get up and go if things get out of hand. Try a restaurant, the park, borrow a meeting space or rent one if necessary.

3. Be prepared: Get control of the facts of your own divorce; understand how the laws of your state apply to the facts; find out the probable outcomes under the law; clarify your goals. You can also prepare by trying to understand your respective emotions and past patterns. Just the fact that you are trying to do this will help make things a little better.

4. Balance the negotiating power:
• If you feel insecure, become informed, be well prepared, use an agenda, get expert advice and guidance. There's never any need to

respond on the spot: state your ideas, listen to your spouse, then think about it until the next meeting. Get advice if you need it; use friends for moral support and venting; then go back in there. Don't meet if you are not calm; don't continue if the meeting doesn't stay business-like. Consider using a professional mediator.

• If you are the stronger spouse, help build your spouse's confidence so he or she can negotiate competently and make sound decisions. Share all information openly with your spouse. Be a good listener: restate what your spouse says to show you heard it; don't respond immediately, just say you'll think about it. Tone yourself back: state your own points clearly but don't try to persuade or "win" a point. Don't argue or repeat yourself. Listen, listen, listen.

5. Build agreement:

• Start with the facts: You should by now have gathered and exchanged all information. If not, complete the information gathering, then try to agree what the facts are. Write down the facts you agree on and list exactly what facts you do not agree on. Note any competing versions then do research to resolve the difference with research and documents. Or compromise—if you can't prove some fact to each other, you may have a hard time proving it in court.

• Make a list of the issues and decisions you *can* agree on. Write them down. This is how you build a foundation for agreement and begin to clarify the major issues between you. Next, write down the things you don't agree on, always trying to refine your differences— to make them more and more clear and precise. Try to break differences down into digestible, bite-sized pieces.

6. Consider needs and interests of both spouses: Avoid taking a position. Consider your needs, interests and concerns alongside the facts of your situation. Work *together* on brainstorming and problem solving; look for ways to satisfy needs and interests of both spouses and try to balance the sacrifices.

7. State issues in a constructive way: Reframing is when you re-state things in a more neutral way, to encourage communication and understanding. For example: One spouse says, "I have to have the house." Reframe: "What I would like most is to have the house, that's my first priority. What the house means to me is....."

8. Get legal advice: Typically, legal questions come up as you negotiate. Get advice; find out if the laws of your state provide a clear, predictable outcome on your particular issue. Don't hesitate to get more than one opinion.

9. Be patient and persistent: Don't rush, don't be in a hurry. Divorces take time and negotiation takes time. Whenever someone hears a new idea, it takes time to percolate. It takes time for people to change their minds. It may take time to shift your mutual orientation from combative to competitive to co-operative. So don't just *do* something; *stand* there! A slow, gradual approach takes pressure off and allows emotions to cool. Meanwhile, you may want to work out temporary solutions for certain issues. If the situation of both spouses is stable and secure for a while, you can afford to take some time. If not, work on that, not the negotiation. Settle in, get as comfortable as you can, go on with building your new life. If the going seems slow, remember, working through attorneys usually takes a *very* long time, many months or even years. You can beat that, for sure.

10. Get help: Negotiating with your spouse may not be easy; you're dealing with old habits, raw wounds, entrenched personality patterns—all the obstacles to agreement all at once. A third person can really help keep things in focus. Mediators are professionals who are specially trained to help you negotiate; they are expert at helping couples get unblocked and into an agreement. Mediation is very effective and it usually goes quickly. In California, you can call Divorce Helpline for help with your negotiation; it's one of the things we do best. Getting help is discussed more in the next sections.

Before you begin to negotiate, give your spouse this book and, if possible, discuss parts of it together. Talk about how you can put these ideas to work and how you can proceed. Go over each step and talk about how it's going and what more can be done. There are many good books about negotiation, but one of the easiest to read is the little (150 page) Penguin paperback by Fisher and Ury, *"Getting to Yes: Negotiating Agreement Without Giving In."* The chapter titles are a check-list for things you need to know:
- Don't bargain over positions
- Separate the people from the problem
- Focus on interests, not positions
- Invent options for mutual gain
- Insist on using objective criteria

- What if they are more powerful?
- What if they won't play?
- What if they use dirty tricks?

After you agree: Chances are very good that you *can* work things out by using the techniques discussed in this book. Once you have reached an agreement, you can relax a little bit, your divorce is effectively over—all that's left is to get it drafted in legally correct form and then go through some red-tape and paperwork to get your Judgment. Read all about how to do this in Chapter 9.

If you can't agree: If you find that working by yourself on getting an agreement isn't working out, don't struggle *too* long; don't wait until you are both at war from entrenched positions; don't get frustrated; don't get depressed; don't get mad—get help.

Mediation and counseling

There are times when a third person (just the right third person) can really help with some well–chosen words of advice, some feedback on how something looks from the outside, another point of view, a new idea for how to handle a situation. When you can't see the forest for the trees, you often get tangled up in tree roots—worse, you get lost. So maybe you should hire a guide.

There are two questions about involving a third person in your divorce. What can you get out of it and who do you go to? In broad terms, there are two kinds of professional help to consider—mediation and counseling. Either one can be extremely useful but the two activities are quite different.

The goal of individual counseling is mental health and emotional growth. A counselor can help you not only to understand and accept yourself, but also to make constructive changes in your habits and attitudes. Counseling can be quite practical and goal-oriented or it can be directed more toward therapy and personal transformation. They help with the difficult job of digging into your own process and dealing with your life. That's what counseling is about. Couples counseling is practical and oriented toward mutual understanding and better communications. This is great stuff if you want to work out an agreement or work on better co-parenting.

To get help, you have to want it. You have to be ready, willing, and able to accept it. One person can get help from counseling, but to mediate, you *both* have to want to do it. You also have to be willing to make full disclosure of all facts and you have to trust that your spouse will not be lying or concealing facts. One of the few disadvantages of mediation compared to court battle is that information cannot be taken under oath.

The goal of mediation is specifically to help a couple reach an agreement. A less popular goal is to bring some order to your disagreements; to narrow and sharpen the issues so if a conflict can't be avoided, it can at least be limited to real issues. This makes any subsequent legal contest more efficient and less expensive.

The mediator is an objective, neutral person who has developed skills specifically targeted on conflict resolution and negotiation. The mediator works to control upset, calm fears, equalize the bargaining power, and keep you focused on needs and interests. A mediator can help you get unstuck by shedding new light, bringing in new ideas, other options. You want either a family law attorney also trained in mediation or a mediator trained in family law. They have to be able to deal with the whole divorce, all the legal and emotional issues at one time.

The mediator works for the couple, not one spouse or the other, and is usually either a family counselor or a lawyer. There are no hard and fast rules, but a counselor might tend to be better at working with the emotional issues and bad communication habits that are the real cause of conflict. Lawyer-mediators will know much more about the laws, likely outcomes of cases, and legal aspects of settlement agreements. Lawyers will usually tend to be more practical, more business-like.

Team mediation is *particularly* effective although it can be more expensive. It uses two mediators, usually a male and a female, one a lawyer and the other a counselor. This way all bases are covered and a richer, safer environment is created for problem solving.

How to get help

You have to be careful who you take advice from, who you let guide you. What if you take bad advice and things don't go well—who pays the price? You do. Advice you do or do not take will have important consequences for the rest of your life. So will words you do or do not say, and choices you do or do not make. So who do you listen to?

112

A lot of people know a little bit and a few people know a lot. You can get advice from friends, relatives, or work-mates—often without even asking for it—but many people don't really know what they are talking about. Something might sound good because it feels comfortable or be-cause you already agree with it or because it comes from someone you know and like, yet still be dead wrong—just plain bad advice.

The person you want to listen to, who can give you the most help, will be objective, neutral, trustworthy, wise and well–informed. They will be very good with people, know what they are doing, and have a lot of experience with a wide variety of divorce scenarios. Sounds like a professional job, doesn't it?

The best way to find professional help is by personal reputation. Licenses and certificates do not guarantee that the practitioner is good or the right person for you. It would be ideal if you could get a recommendation from someone you know and trust who has used a certain professional for a divorce with good results. That's asking a lot, so let's assume you are just shopping around. Here are some things to consider:

• Try to get a recommendation from someone reliable. Talk to other professionals in related fields or call on local divorce support groups. If nothing else, look in the yellow pages under Divorce Assistance, Attorneys, Mediators, or Counselors.
• Interview more than one prospective professional.
• Ask about their fee schedule.
• Ask about their training and background. Are they licensed? How long have they been in business? Do they do it full-time? Are they well-established locally?
• Ask about their area of expertise, how much experience they have had, and what other services they provide. You want someone who has a lot of experience.
• Ask what their goals are and try to get a sense of the style and approach they use in cases like yours.
• Do they ask you questions, too, to find out if their service is the most appropriate? Do they explain what they do and do they distinguish mediation from counseling, or their type of counseling from other approaches?

- Does their work place feel calm and private?
- Do they discuss your options with you?

Finally, the most important thing to consider is not a rational process at all—the person you work with has to *feel* right to you. Mediation and counseling are intensely personal. Whatever it is that works happens on the level of personalities—yours and theirs. You need to find a professional with strength of character, experience, wisdom, and a personality that suits you. Without these, not all the techniques and education in the world will do the trick.

What if you can't agree?

After all our talk about the advantages of reaching agreement, it is finally time to face the fact that you can't always get one no matter what you do. Or maybe working with your spouse on an agreement is not something you want to do under any circumstances. Maybe you just want what you are entitled to and that's all.

It all amounts to the same thing. If you can't settle, you have to battle. If you have to battle, you may as well learn how to do it in the most efficient and cost-effective way possible—and while you're at it, learn how to minimize the damage to yourself and to your children. So move on to Chapter 10 and join the Battle Group.

9

How to Do Your Own Divorce
—cases with no legal opposition

You should read this chapter no matter how much disagreement or conflict there is in your case. It will help you understand one of the primary pay-offs for working hard to settle disagreements—that is, how easy it is to complete an unopposed case.

How to keep an easy case easy

Many cases start out unopposed, but it's never a surprise if what seems to be an unopposed case flares up into conflict. Fortunately, there are things you can do if this happens to you. The techniques you use to deal with flare-ups are the same ones you use to quiet and settle a case that starts out conflicted. This is covered in Chapter 8 where we discuss how to reduce conflict.

Be sure your spouse has a copy of this book. Give one to him or her if necessary—it can only help. That way, you will *both* have good information and maybe you can talk about things that concern you in terms of the ideas and solutions suggested here.

Doing your own divorce

What we've been talking about all along in this book is Doing Your Own Divorce. You've already been doing it; you are doing it right now. Doing your own divorce does *not* mean filling out divorce forms, though you can choose to do that if you want to. It does *not* mean typing up your own agreement, though you may be able to do that, too, if you have a relatively simple estate. What is important is that you work out your own terms outside the legal system without retaining an attorney to take over your case. *That's* doing your own divorce.

Studies have shown that a good divorce outcome is related to the degree of involvement and participation of both spouses. The more you can do yourselves, the better off you will be—and that's a scientifically proven fact.

The mechanics of doing a divorce are relatively simple, once it's clear that your case is uncontested. You may well wonder why lawyers charge so much for doing them. If you take care of things yourself, even if you hire help, you'll be better off *and* save money *and* reduce the chance of getting tangled up in the legal system.

There are two kinds of cases that can be handled as uncontested:
• if you and your spouse have reached an agreement on all issues, at any point in the legal process; or
• you don't have an agreement but there will be no legal opposition from your spouse anyway. Typically, this happens when there is no marital property or debts, no kids, and no need for support; or where there will be no legal opposition because your spouse is long gone, or just doesn't care.

What has to get done: To complete an uncontested case, you have only one or two steps to get your divorce:
Draft your agreement. If your case will be uncontested because you have an agreement, your agreement has to be drafted in a legally sound form, the marital settlement agreement (MSA), then you sign it;
Complete the paperwork. In every uncontested divorce, with or without an agreement, you have to go through some paperwork and red-tape to get your Judgment.

Cases with agreements

If you are negotiating your own agreement, you will want to get the details of the agreement worked out and stated very clearly in an informal writing before you make the formal marital settlement agreement. There are two basic approaches for doing this: the Memo of Understanding, or the more formal Proposed Agreement. The primary difference is style; use one or both, whatever works.

These informal writings are not intended to be a binding contract. You don't *want* to make a binding contract at this point because you might get it wrong or one of you might have a change of mind. In early stages of divorce negotiations, especially if emotions are still running high, it's not unusual to have a change of mind and it takes a lot of pressure off the negotiations if both

116

parties know it's okay to rethink and renegotiate decisions. It is much better to renegotiate now rather than litigate later over a hasty agreement. When you write down terms in your memo or proposal, be sure to use clear, specific language and be as thorough, detailed and complete as possible.

Memo of Understanding: While negotiating with your spouse, whenever you reach any agreement, even a partial or temporary one, make a memo of what you have agreed to as soon as possible, right on the spot if you can. Put a heading, "Memo of Understanding" at the top and start with, "Our current understanding of our agreement is as follows:" then you write down the terms, sign it and each keep a copy. The memo of understanding is a record of the current stage of your negotiation and it eventually becomes the worksheet for drafting a legal and binding marital settlement agreement.

Proposed Agreement: A different style is for the spouses to send each other written proposed terms to be considered or discussed. The heading is, "Proposed Terms," and you begin with something like, "I propose we settle on the following terms." Keep exchanging proposals and discussing the points until you reach terms that you can both approve.

Once your agreement is stable, complete and settled, you next get it drawn up (drafted) in the form of a legally correct marital settlement agreement. Then you sign it. *Then* it is binding.

If a lot of property is involved, one or both of you may want to see a lawyer—perhaps the same lawyer at the same time—before you sign a binding agreement. This is to make sure you understand every aspect of the agreement and haven't left out anything important or inadvertently used wording that won't work. Let the lawyer improve the wording and raise other considerations, but don't let anyone talk you out of the agreements you have made without getting at least one other opinion.

How to do it. How does your agreement get turned into a legal document that works? Well, you either do it yourself or you get professional help. Remember, the terms of your marital settlement agreement (MSA) will become the terms of your Judgment, so you want to get it done exactly right. The MSA may be the most important transaction of your life, financially and personally, so you want to know it's legally sound. Drafting an MSA is a very technical craft. The language has to be excellent and unambiguous so you don't have two possible interpretations of any term. It has to be complete and legally correct, otherwise it might be weak or defective. If some legal requirement is overlooked, it might not work correctly.

Can you safely draft your MSA entirely by yourself or should you get help? The answer is, what have you got to lose?
- If you haven't got much property or income, then you haven't got much to lose by doing everything yourself. You can't afford much help anyway, so you'll have to struggle along the best you can on your own.
- If you have enough income or property to worry about, it may not be a good idea to draft your own MSA—you need to make sure everything is done right and it's probably worth it for you to get some help. Here's one way to think about it: add up the value of all your property and add to that the amount of all your debts then add the value of all future support payments. Compare that figure with the cost of professional help and a divorce that is done right.

The sample agreement in Appendix A can help you think of terms to discuss and language to use in your informal writing. Resources and services you can use to get your agreement drafted are discussed below in the section, "Where to find help?"

Red tape and paperwork

By the time you sign your agreement, you may already have started your divorce with a Petition, or maybe you have yet to begin your legal divorce. Either way, you have more red-tape to go through.

Can you do the red-tape and paperwork yourself? Yes, you absolutely can—if there is a reliable book or kit for your state. (See below, "Where to find help?") Hundreds of thousands of people do it themselves every year using books and kits that are specifically for their state. It's not *really* difficult, not exactly, not much worse than doing your own income tax the first time. But it can be very tedious and a very big bother.

Should you get professional help? Ask yourself two questions:
- can you afford to pay a few hundred dollars?
- what else could you be doing with your time?

If you can afford it, it would probably be better to get someone else to take care of the red-tape and paperwork for you. Give yourself a treat; get this load off your shoulders. You'd be better off spending the time on yourself, visiting your kids, building yourself a new life. On the other hand, maybe you'd rather have a paperwork hobby for awhile.

Where to find help

Books: Start by looking for a good self-help book on the divorce laws of your state. Nolo Press publishes the famous *How to Do Your Own Divorce* books in California and Texas. For other states, go to a book store or library and search the *Books In Print* subject matter catalog under "Divorce," where you will find a section of state-by-state listings. Most states have self-help divorce books but it may not be easy to tell how good or how accurate they are. The worst thing would be an old book that has not kept up with changes, so check the date of printing. Ask the reference librarian or store personnel to make recommendations. If you can find a good one, this may be all you need. You decide.

Paralegals and divorce typing services: Another way that lawyerless divorces get done is with the help of a divorce typing service, sometimes called paralegals. The theory is that you know exactly what you want and merely hire secretarial assistance to prepare and process your paperwork.

No formal training is required to run a divorce typing service, so don't expect reliable legal advice. It is important that *you* be informed and know exactly what you want. It would not be safe to have a divorce typing service draft any but the simplest marital settlement agreement unless you have a fairly simple, low value case and your MSA is just like one in a reliable divorce book or kit for your state.

Most paralegals or divorce typing services keep ads running in the personal classified section of their local newspapers or in the yellow pages under "Divorce Assistance" or some similar heading. Before you hire someone, find out how long they have been in business, talk to them, ask for references and really check them out.

Divorce Helpline: In California, the best help you can get is from Divorce Helpline. This is a new kind of law firm that exists only to help people get themselves through divorce. Their attorneys are expert at helping people solve problems and reach settlement. Working throughout California by mail, phone, and fax, they offer legal information, advice, help with negotiations and mediation. They will also draft marital settlement agreements and do your paperwork for you. The best thing is that they offer fixed fees for services and they will work with both spouses if you want them to. If you are in California, call 1-800-359-7004.

Lawyers: You may, of course, decide to have a lawyer handle your divorce from start to finish. Many people still do. This costs a *lot* more but may be necessary in cases with unavoidable conflict or a very high degree of complexity. Take care that lawyerly techniques do not increase the conflict or complexity of your case, and that you get no more legal action than you really need. Be prepared, know what's going on, supervise and manage your own case. That's what works best. You can also hire an attorney just to draft your MSA. This kind of job should be done at a flat rate; call around and compare prices.

In some cities, there are cheap lawyers who run divorce mills but, here as anywhere, you frequently get what you pay for. If they do not complicate your case and promote more legal work for themselves, they will essentially be doing the work of a divorce typist for a higher price. Cheap lawyers can't take the time to help you understand your case; they are notorious for not returning your calls. If they get into a conflict with a well-paid attorney, they can't keep up the same level of attention and will be working your case at a disadvantage.

You should only hire a family law specialist, and preferably one who is also a professional mediator. Read Chapter 11 about choosing and using a lawyer.

Foreign divorces: If anyone offers to sell you a fast, cheap divorce from the Dominican Republic, or anywhere else outside of your state, and if they say you don't have to live there or even go there, you should be *extremely* suspicious. Foreign divorces that can be bought without either spouse going there are probably not worth the price of the paper and they definitely can't be used to get valid orders concerning property, child custody or support.

How to Win a Controlled Legal Battle

If you have to fight, you might as well learn how to do it effectively, so welcome to the Battle Group. Notice that the chapter title says "legal" battle—you do not *need* to battle on a personal or emotional level in order to win a legal battle. Notice that the title says "controlled" battle—people hardly ever win an *un*controlled battle. This chapter is where you learn how to control a legal battle when you can't (or don't want to) avoid one, how to battle efficiently and effectively, and how to minimize the damage.

How to deal with extreme conflict

Is your spouse violent? Alcoholic? A *terrible* nuisance? In extreme cases of harassment or violence there are legal remedies and there are practical things that you can and *must* do for yourself. This is not about how to reach agreement—these are strategies for self-defense. Mental and physical abuse must never be tolerated.

Restraining orders: The legal remedy for domestic harassment and violence is a restraining order—an order from the court, served personally on your spouse, forbidding certain conduct. Restraining orders are available in any divorce (see Chapter 6— keeping the peace). Where there has been physical harm to you or your children or where future harm is threatened, you can go to court to have your spouse ordered to move out and stay away from the family residence. Child visitation can be ordered for specific times and places, away from your home, or, in bad cases, under supervision. It takes very clear proof of danger or detriment to the child to forbid visitation altogether. In extreme cases where there is clear evidence of imminent danger, some states permit orders to be issued *ex parte*—without notice to or participation of your spouse—which are binding only until a hearing can be held and more orders issued after hearing both sides. You should retain an attorney to get your restraining orders.

Here's the good news: over 85% of all restraining orders are adhered to. Being served with orders from a court seems to have a good effect on most abusers, and, more to the point, they now know that you are serious about not being a victim. Is your spouse the kind of person that will respect a court order? Will he or she care about the police coming out or being dragged into court and talked to sternly by a judge? Does your spouse have a reputation, money or property to protect? Will your spouse, in the heat of rage or hatred, ignore the threat or reality of police presence?

When you request restraining orders as part of your divorce action, you can also take that opportunity to request temporary orders for support, custody, or visitation that will set the terms of your separation until a full-scale trial is held or a settlement is reached. Temporary orders can be very useful if you need them to stabilize your case or get support coming in.

Police: If you have a restraining order, be sure to file it with your local police. This can put them under extra pressure to protect you. But whether you have court orders or not, don't hesitate to call the police if you are the victim of serious domestic harassment or violence, and *keep* calling them. At the very least, you will be building a case and developing evidence.

You should be aware of the practical realities of police intervention. The police may be an unreliable source of help in domestic situations, although this will vary from place to place. They have been accused of prejudice and sexism, but whether or not that is true, their conduct is also based on years of frustrating and dangerous experience. Police are much more likely to get hurt and less likely to do any real good in domestic disputes than in any other kind of case. This difficult issue has received a great deal of public attention, so police agencies now tend to have standards for dealing with domestic violence. Some departments have officers specially trained in family crisis intervention. Ask responding officers if they can refer you to available spouse abuse shelters, support groups or relevant community services agencies. Call your local police, talk to them about your problem and see what their attitude is and in what way they are willing to help. Start a record in their files.

Self-help and other practical considerations: The best kind of help is the help you give yourself. The only thing you can control in life is your own attitude, actions and reactions, so start there. What part do you play in provocation or in being a victim? Try to avoid the kinds of things that set your spouse off. This does *not* mean to give up and roll over, but it does mean learning to express yourself cleanly and not to provoke. In most disturbed relationships, there is some pattern of action and reaction that builds to an eruption. Try to understand your part and stop the cycle.

Don't be a victim. Spouse abuse is a *very* common problem so you are not unique or alone. Nearly every community has professionals, agencies, and family support groups that have a lot of special knowledge and experience with domestic conflict. They can almost certainly help you. To find a local support group, ask a pastor, call the police department or a social services agency. If one group isn't what you want, try another. Maybe you can get help from friends and family, possibly have someone move in with you for a while, or get a roommate (a big one). One obvious practical solution is to move away, either for good or at least until things cool down. Or change all the locks, bar the windows and get an unlisted phone number. Or get a big dog. Or take self-defense classes. If necessary, hide—it may be better than being someone's easy target. The main thing is this: do whatever you must to create your own peace and safety; do *not* depend solely on police or court orders to solve your problem.

Damage control

Have you already read above about how expensive a legal battle is and how emotionally destructive it can be? It is all true. You should never get into a legal battle if you can possibly avoid it. On the other hand, you should not surrender your rights or your self respect in order to avoid a fight. If you end up in a battle, it is essential that you understand what you are getting into, then do everything possible to minimize the damage and protect yourself and your children.

Commercial airlines are required by law to tell parents they must always put on their own oxygen mask first, then take care of their children. You can't help a child if you pass out in the process. Same with divorce; you have to be okay before you can help anyone else. So, the first thing you do to protect your kids from harm in a divorce battle is to protect yourself—to develop and maintain your own sense of well-being.

Protecting yourself
The issues in a divorce conflict are almost always emotional ones that get played out in terms of property, money and children. As a

tool of emotional warfare, the legal battle is the ultimate button a spouse can push; the same kind of decision that can launch armies or the ultimate missiles. *You are inviting terrible harm to yourself to whatever extent your legal battle is an extension of the emotional conflict you have been conducting with your mate all along.*

The most effective technique is for you to *keep business and emotions separate.* As far as you should be concerned, a divorce battle is strictly a matter of business. It should be run strictly according to reason and practical considerations. If your spouse gets confused and trapped into an emotional conflict, don't react; don't get involved in it at that level. If your spouse or your spouse's attorney use tactics that are upsetting, don't give them the satisfaction of letting it work on that level. Go back and take a look at the suggestions in Chapter 4 for keeping the divorce on a business level.

To survive a legal battle with minimum damage, you *must* free yourself *unilaterally* from the old patterns that you and your mate were trapped in. Never mind what your spouse does or says—that's not your concern now; your job is to get out of it from *your* end. That means dismantling a part of your own internal process. Psychological traps like self-blame or blaming your spouse (see Chapter 3) are like cement blocks on your legs—they will drag you down for sure. You have to free yourself from the old emotional battle and conduct your legal battle as a piece of business.

The check-list for what you have to do to minimize emotional damage to yourself is like an incantation or a prayer that can protect you. Repeat this over and over to yourself as you prepare for battle:

> "I will do what's right, I will do what I must, I will do what
> I can, and I will do my best, but I will *not* worry about the
> rest—it is out of my hands and my well-being does not
> depend on it."

Do what's right: To get through a battle relatively unscathed, you will need the strength that comes from a clear conscience and moral certainty.
 • You must be certain that you want only what is rightfully yours and what is best for the children. Is what you want within the range of probable outcomes—is it *clearly* supported by the

124

facts and the rules of law? Be *sure* to get more than one lawyer's opinion before you fight.

• You must be very clear that you are not acting out of anger, guilt, fear or greed—that you are not seeking revenge, not trying to punish or control your spouse. You must be certain that you are not merely continuing the old emotional conflict.

You will be protected from emotional damage by the strength that comes from knowing in your heart that what you are doing is right and unavoidable—that you have made every effort to be flexible. Without this, the legal battle can turn your life into pure hell.

Do what you must: You must know that you have done everything in your power to avoid this battle. It should be perfectly clear that in order to protect your rights, you have exhausted all other alternatives and have no better choice than to go to the lawyers and courts. On the other hand, you should never just roll-over and give in just to have it done with. You should never feel guilty for insisting on your rights or for refusing to sacrifice your self-respect.

Do what you can: We all live within the limitations of what is possible. There is no blame for failing to achieve any goal, only for failing to make the effort and to use whatever talents and resources that are available to you. If you have a right or a child to protect or some dignity to preserve and you fail to make the effort, then you have not done what you can.

Do your best: You can't control others, you can't control most events, you can only do your best. Like everyone else out there, you are an imperfect and fallible human being, so there's no sense in punishing yourself if you occasionally fall short of perfection. If things don't go your way, you don't have to blame yourself if you know that you gave it your best effort. Instead, give yourself a reward and take some credit for your good intentions and for having tried so hard.

Don't worry about the rest: If you do what's right, what you must, what you can, and give it your best, you will discharge all personal obligations in the matter. This is like the ancient practice of writing troubles and prayers on paper that you then cast into a river. You have committed your case into the unfathomable processes of the legal system, so the matter is out of your hands and the outcome is no longer in your control. There's no point in worrying about it or being attached to it.

Whenever you get caught up in conflict or feel ground down by it, repeat this a few times: "I have done what's right, I did what I had to, I did what I could, and I have done my best, so I will *not* worry about the rest—it's out of my hands and I don't depend on it."

It is very important to adopt an attitude and a life-style that does not depend on the outcome of the battle or on anything your spouse says or does. This doesn't mean you shouldn't care about it or try your best, but don't let your well-being depend on the outcome. While the legal battle drags on—and it may be quite a long time—you should explore other avenues and build a foundation out of the other resources in your life. The legal wheel is turning and the chips may or may not come to you when it stops. Meanwhile, get on with building your life.

Protecting your children

Go back and read page 36, "Rules of the Road #2—Getting Your Children Through a Tough Time."

Studies show that harm to children is more closely related to conflict *after* the divorce. Everyone has conflict before and during a divorce, but if you want to protect your children, get finished with the conflict and resolve it, at least within yourself, as quickly as possible.

Children need their relationship with both parents. There is a bonding that cannot easily be replaced by a surrogate parent or step-parent. To protect the essential parent-child relationship, you have to insulate children from your own conflict with their other parent. The divorce is not their problem; it's yours. Being a bad wife or husband does not make your spouse a bad parent. So, don't hold the children hostage—they are not pawns or bartering pieces in your game. In the area of custody and visitation, don't bargain with your spouse on any other basis than what will give your children the most stability and the best contact with both parents.

The worst thing for the child of a broken home is feeling responsible for the break-up and feeling that loving one parent is a betrayal of the other. These feelings cause children intense stress and insecurity. To protect your child from almost unbearable pain, don't say anything bad about the other parent in front of the child; don't undermine or interfere in any way with the child's relationship with or love for the other parent; don't put the child in a position of having to take sides. Do encourage every possible kind of constructive relationship your child can have with your ex-mate. Let the children know that you are happy when they have a good, loving time with their other parent.

Kids can really get on your nerves at a time like this and single parenting is enough to overwhelm any normal person. You are not Superman or Mary Marvel and kids are not designed to be raised by one lone person. You need help and support, and you need time off from the kids. Make a point of getting help from family, friends and the many parent support groups and family service agencies throughout the United States. Get references to groups in your area through temples, churches or social service agencies.

Winning strategies—hardball or softball?

What does "winning" mean to you? Think about it. You have certain goals to pursue and rights to protect—that's all. The first and most important thing you do to "win" is to immediately stop thinking about winning and your spouse losing. Divorce isn't that kind of contest and a relationship is not a battlefield. If you think that way, you are setting yourself up to be a loser. Separate yourself from the contest emotionally and conduct this strictly as a piece of business.

Never start a divorce contest on the strength of a single opinion. Take your case around for a variety of advice. This is essential: don't skimp at this critical step in your case. Ask your lawyer: are your demands reasonable under the law? Ask yourself: are your goals worth the price of the battle?

What *are* your goals for this legal contest? Whatever your other goals, there is one that should always have top priority—to *negotiate* an acceptable settlement. Everything you and your attorney do should be aimed at getting your spouse and your spouse's attorney into good-faith negotiations that will lead to an agreement that you can both accept. Okay, what strategy do you use to do that?

There are two basic types of divorce strategy, defensive and aggressive. Which should you use? Well, when anxious hikers asked what to do if they ran into a bear, the old woodsman

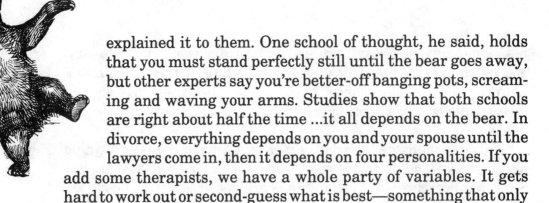

explained it to them. One school of thought, he said, holds that you must stand perfectly still until the bear goes away, but other experts say you're better-off banging pots, screaming and waving your arms. Studies show that both schools are right about half the time ...it all depends on the bear. In divorce, everything depends on you and your spouse until the lawyers come in, then it depends on four personalities. If you add some therapists, we have a whole party of variables. It gets hard to work out or second-guess what is best—something that only gets clear after it's all over.

Hardball or softball? Softball is a civilized, easy-going approach to the legal contest. Your purpose is only to stick to what you think is right and, if necessary, let some judge decide. It is a decision to disagree peacefully, to let the lawyers do their job and the legal process take its course. If you can't agree, why get upset? Let the judge decide. Hardball, on the other hand, is a tough, aggressive strategy. If your spouse is being bad or is likely to cheat, you have to defend your rights very forcefully—and you might have to show some teeth. If your spouse is the one who starts being legally aggressive, you have a choice—respond in kind or be defensive.

Aggressive cases are those in which you are on the offensive. You move fast; you hire an aggressive lawyer to take the legal field and strike hard. You fire off a full range of legal motions and go to hearings to freeze accounts, put your spouse under court orders to behave, and set rigid visitation schedules for children. You send out volumes of legal interrogatories (questions) and you demand or subpoena boxes of documents and paperwork. Aggression costs a great deal of money and can destroy future hopes for good personal and co-parenting relationships. It can damage your children, maybe permanently. But, in extreme cases, it might be necessary.

One goal might be to get what you have been denied: honest information, your fair share of the community property, access to your children, relief from abuse, and the like. Another goal may be to make a dramatic statement to your mate—a cold splash of legal realism as shock therapy. You are showing teeth in the hopes that it will lead to negotiation. However, aggression is risky business that can back-fire. It depends on the temperament of your spouse *and* your spouse's attorney. Avoid the trap of using legal aggression to punish or harass your spouse—that sword cuts two ways and you *will* get hurt. It isn't worth it. You should use aggression only if forced into it by circumstances beyond your control.

To conduct an aggressive case, you will be looking for an aggressive lawyer who is also experienced, bright, tough, and tenacious. Spend some time interviewing various lawyers about their philosophies and attitudes. If, for example, a lawyer is *eager* to attack, that lawyer may be just as quick to attack you if a difference of opinion arises. Look for someone who goes to battle reluctantly, who is always looking for a way to cool the battle down, but who can punch it out if necessary. Read more about choosing your lawyer in Chapter 11.

Defensive cases are those where your spouse is on the attack and is coming on hard and strong. Don't get mad; this is business. Your choice here is either to conduct a stubborn defense or to go on the offensive. If you do the least possible to protect your position, you conserve your energy and money while waiting for your mate's team to run out of steam. A quiet defense may make it easier to negotiate an agreement later. A good defense is almost always more comfortable and less expensive. Let them do the work; let them bark and growl; you can just rely on the facts and the legal process.

If your mate's attorney is unusually aggressive or if they play dirty tricks, like making the case unnecessarily expensive with a flood of paperwork and motions in court, you may decide to play their game. If you counter-attack and drag your mate personally through some depositions and hearings, maybe you'll convince your mate to negotiate. But first, ask some questions or yourself and of your attorney:

- Have they got the facts right?
- Does the law support their position?
- Are they aiming anywhere near the probable outcome?
- Is your mate's position or personality vulnerable somewhere?
- Is this going to be worth the expense?
- What's the advantage of striking back compared to just letting it go to court? What do you have to gain? What can you lose?

The strategy you decide to use always depends on knowing very clearly what your goals are, then you consider the facts and circumstances, and the personalities of the people—you, your spouse, your attorneys. Then you make your decisions and choices.

Obviously, softball is the better game. It costs less and hurts less. If you don't have to worry about bad or dishonest behavior, let the lawyers negotiate and the judge decide what can't be agreed.

Even if you get into an aggressive battle, you should always be looking for ways to cool it down and to negotiate an agreement.

How to fight effectively at less expense

1—Know exactly what you want from the battle

The most important part of preparation for battle is thought. Don't go to war without it. Think about your case, your life, and get very detailed and specific about what you want: property, support, future relationships for yourself and your children, life goals and values. Sometimes all you want at first is more information that your spouse won't give you, or a check on what has been given. Your lawyer can get information under oath. At some point, you will have all the information there is, then you will have to decide finally what you ultimately want.

Planning your battle strategy—even to the type of attorney you choose—depends on a clear understanding of what you want to accomplish in the battle. What property do you want? How much support? How much do you care about future relations between you and your spouse or the emotional well-being of your children and their relationship with their other parent?

2—Try to narrow the issues

Before you get into a battle and all during the fight, do whatever you can to narrow the issues. This means you try to agree with your spouse, in writing, to as many points as possible. Sometimes you can agree to a whole lot of things, then agree that you disagree on certain remaining issues and that you will let the court decide. A battle is much more efficient when conducted on a narrow front. Be very cautious about taking advice to broaden the battle! It may indeed strengthen your bargaining position if you ask far more than you want or attack an issue you don't care about, but it can also stimulate the opposition, undermine your credibility, and prolong the battle.

3—Set the tone of the battle

If you care at all about keeping the level of conflict as low as possible, then be sure to keep your spouse informed at all times and well ahead of time about what you and your lawyer are doing and why you are doing it. This helps to minimize unpleasant surprises,

130

misunderstandings and over-reaction, especially if your spouse returns the favor. It helps to keep the background lines of communications open. Communicate by letter to avoid arguments; keep copies. Remember, most cases eventually get settled by the spouses between themselves, not by their lawyers, so you will be better off for trying to keep communication lines open.

4—Carefully choose the right lawyer
It may be okay to rely on the first attorney you interview for information, but that's not good enough for a battle. It is *very* important to take your case around to several lawyers to get a variety of opinions and attitudes before you choose the one you want. Don't economize at the wrong time; paying for these extra interviews can save you a fortune later. Read Chapter 11, think about your objectives, then decide what lawyer you are going to work with.

5—Be thoroughly prepared and informed
When you go to see a lawyer, you don't want to waste any time—it costs too much. You should know your goals, be familiar with all facts of your case, and know as specifically as possible what you want to talk about with the attorney. Send the attorney a note before you go in, detailing exactly what you want to discuss, and include copies of any relevant documents. That gives the lawyer time to absorb your information and gives you a chance to see if the lawyer bothers to prepare for the conference.

Organize your papers and your thoughts; make an agenda before you go in. Keep notes on every discussion; keep track of time spent on the phone or in the office so you can compare it to the itemized billing.

6—Make it clear that you are in charge of your case
This is your life and you have to live with any consequences of the divorce action, so it is reasonable—and important—that you be ultimately in charge of your own case. You want to hire the lawyer's knowledge and experience; you very much want to listen to the lawyer's good advice; but you expect to be part of any decisions that affect the tone and strategy of the case. You will be ultimately responsible.

Tell the lawyer that you would like copies of all papers and correspondence, and that you expect to be kept informed of every step in the action. Also make it clear that you expect your phone calls to be returned as soon as possible, no later than the next working day. In return, you have to reassure the lawyer that you will not be one of those clients that makes frivolous calls.

7—Don't hesitate to switch attorneys
If your attorney's services turn out to be unsatisfactory, you should send a letter with specific details of what the problem is and what changes you want made. If there is no improvement, start looking for another attorney. See Chapter 11 on firing an attorney.

How to Choose and Use a Lawyer

Shopping for an attorney is like shopping for melons; you should check the prices and make sure the one you choose "feels" right to you. You have a right to ask questions, look things over and be choosy about whom you hire for such an important role in your life.

Don't be intimidated. Call around to find out how much it will cost just to meet the lawyer and see if you want to hire him or her. Ask what the hourly rate is (and if there is a flat fee if you have an uncontested case). If you want help with just one specific part of doing your own divorce (say, a marital settlement agreement) ask if they will do this and at what rate. Most attorneys do the initial interview for nothing or a fairly small fee. Rates run from $80 to $500 per hour, but $150 to $350 is quite common and will be higher in cities and lower in suburban or rural areas.

Before you see the attorney, be sure you are thoroughly prepared with the facts of your case and know exactly what you want to talk about. Have copies of all relevant documents and information ready. You might consider mailing the information in ahead of time so the attorney will have a chance to be prepared, too. Few attorneys will spend much time preparing for an initial interview, especially if they charge little or nothing for it. However, it can do no harm and it will show that you are business-like and thorough.

You want three things in your divorce attorney: expertise in divorce, reliability, and a good attitude. You want a lawyer who specializes in divorce (at least 50% of their case load) and you are strongly advised to find a lawyer trained in divorce mediation who practices it professionally. Mediation-minded attorneys are more likely to give you neutral and problem-solving advice, whereas traditional attorneys tend to be more oriented to conflict and their advice tends to be adversarial. Your attorney must be someone you can trust and work with comfortably, someone who has your confidence.

The best way to find a good divorce lawyer is on the recommendation of another professional (say, a divorce counselor) who has reason to know about divorce attorneys and their reputations. The next best way is on the personal recommendation of someone you know well and trust who has had a divorce and been pleased with a particular lawyer's services. Finally, your local bar association will have a referral service; look them up in the yellow pages and ask for a family law specialist. Be very cautious with recommendations from people you do not know and especially where the service they had was not a divorce. It is not useful to know that a certain attorney is good at business, personal injury, or criminal work when what you want is a divorce.

In some states, the Bar certifies family law specialists. The specialist has taken the trouble to get extra professional training and sit for qualifying exams, and has shown a special interest in family law practice. Of course, many general practitioners are also excellent and well-qualified in the divorce arena. All things being equal, it would be better to have a family law specialist, so start shopping in that category. But all things are *not* equal: knowledge and experience are very important, but attitude sits right at the top of any list and you can't get a certificate for it.

It is extremely difficult to judge a lawyer's technical competence, so for that you will have to rely on the State Bar's specialist certification program, personal references and reputation. When shopping for attitude, it helps to know that there are several distinct types of divorce lawyers, distinguished by their attitudes on three key subjects: attitude toward the client, attitude toward therapists and counselors, and goals of legal activity. Below is a list based on lawyer types suggested in Ken Kressel's scholarly book, *The Process of Divorce*.

A field guide to divorce lawyer types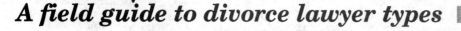

Here are three innocent questions that you should sprinkle through your first interview. Ask the attorney:

- What are your goals in this kind of case; what will you try to accomplish?
- What do you think is a good outcome for a divorce case?
- How do you feel about working with counselors, mediators, and therapists?

The way the attorney responds will reveal a lot about his or her attitude and will help you locate the attorney in the guide below. This is not fool-proof (especially if they have read this book) since lawyers are professional at showing the face they want you to see. Ultimately, you will be relying on your instincts.

1. The Cynic

This lawyer does not respect his client (or very many people, for that matter). Thinks his or her job is thankless and messy, and that the clients are emotionally unbalanced. Cynical about human nature generally, pessimistic that a good or constructive outcome is ever possible in divorce. Sometimes derogatory toward clients, especially behind their backs. Skeptical about the value of counseling; may refer clients to counseling, but mostly to get rid of the burden. Committed to helping a client "win" whatever they want. Dislikes disruption of schedules due to counselor's advice to wait. This one is hard to spot—rarely lets it show.

2. The Gallant Gladiator

Also known as a "hired gun," "mechanic," or "technician." Pragmatic and technical. Assumes clients are capable of knowing what they want. Thinks the lawyer's job is to evaluate the feasibility of the clients goals, then go for it. Unlike the Cynic, does not disparage clients. Thinks a good outcome is possible —"good" meaning to produce results for the client. Views counselors according to usefulness for evidence, as expert witnesses.

3. The Tiger/ Pugilist

An extreme variant of the cynic (the pugilist) or the gladiator (the tiger). Mauls the other side with a continuous barrage of motions, demands and legal maneuvers. Might intentionally be offensive to opposing attorneys; seeks to upset and wear down the opposition, to grind them into submission. Tiger thrives on the hunt, pugilist is just a thug. Dangerous to associate with as they may bite the hand that used to feed them.

4. The Mediator

Oriented toward compromise, negotiation, and rational problem solving. Emphasizes cooperation with the other side, particularly the other attorney. Appeals to client's better nature and assumes client wants "what's fair." Posture of emotional neutrality. Unlike the above types, tends to downplay (but not deny) the adversarial nature of lawyer's role. Fights only when provoked by the other side. May refuse to carry out aggressive, conflict oriented demands of client. A good outcome is one both parties can live with. Uses counselors to de-escalate conflict.

5. The Social Worker

Concerned for client's over all well-being, post-divorce adjustment, and (especially for females) employability. Keeps entire family in mind and concerned about long-range plans for children (camps, education, etc.) Sees that divorce is not usually an easy solution to marital unhappiness, but without the pessimism or rancor of the Cynic. Unlike above types, sees reconciliation as a professional obligation, not a waste of time. Has some enthusiasm for therapy, welcomes counselors in any stage of proceedings. Good outcome is one where client achieves social reintegration. Believes that social services and institutions for divorced families need to be expanded.

6. The Therapist

Accepts that client is in a state of emotional stress and turmoil. Assumes legal aspects can be adequately dealt with only by engaging the emotional ones; tries to understand client's motivation. Gets involved with reconciliation. Sees a good outcome as reintegration of client. Welcomes involvement of counselors. Thinks legal system not adequate for people's needs in divorce. Committed to reducing conflict wherever possible. Opposes belligerent, vengeful demands of client. Aware of tunnel–vision from getting only one side of the conflict, but still subject to it; frustrated by professional ethics prohibiting contact with the other spouse; tries round-about means to get insight into the other side.

7. The Moralist

Rejects neutrality, does not hesitate to use own sense of right and wrong. Gets involved. Will oppose client's demands when felt to be "right" and necessary. May aggressively address client's stance and try to "correct" client's attitude. Really strong about children; may demand client send child to counselor. Whether the Moralist's view is based on sound understanding of people or psychology is open to question. Good outcome is what satisfies the lawyer's sense of fair play, parental duties, right and wrong.

Questions to ask a lawyer

In addition to the questions suggested above about the lawyer's attitude and goals, you will want to ask:

About the attorney's background—
- how long have you been in practice?
- how long with this firm?
- what areas of law do you specialize in?
- what percentage of your practice is divorce?
- what percentage of your divorce cases settle without *any* formal legal action (that is, motions or discovery)?
- do you practice as a professional divorce mediator?
- what percentage of your case load is mediation?

About fees—
- how much do you charge? If you want a specific service, there may be a flat fee—so much, say, for a marital settlement agreement. Otherwise, it is likely to be an hourly rate. Either way, get it clear.
- how am I billed for your secretary's time or research by other staff?
- what costs can we anticipate?
- how much do you need to get started?
- is the initial retainer to be applied against future billings?
- if the retainer exceeds the billings, will the balance be returned?
- can I count on you to get your fee from my spouse, or am I going to be responsible for your payment and collection from my spouse?
- do you bill exactly for time spent, say for short phone calls, or do you round-off to a higher time period?

About other things—
- can I expect a copy of all papers and documents?
- do you need any information that you don't have yet?
- based on my facts, do you see any problems in this case?

Who to pick?

If you want advice, be sure to look for a mediator/attorney, as explained at the beginning of this chapter. If you want an appraisal of likely outcomes in your local courts, or drafting of a marital settlement agreement, then you are mostly concerned with the attorney's knowledge and experience. Attitude is less relevant here, as you are handling your own case. But watch out for the attorney who seems to make things more confused rather than less, or who urges you to do things that could lead to conflict.

If you want an attorney to handle your divorce for you, the person you choose has a lot to do with your strategy and the current temperature of relations with your spouse. We suggest that you generally avoid anyone who seems cynical, unnecessarily aggressive, or moralistic. For most cases, you will want to look for someone who prefers to avoid conflict in favor of negotiation and compromise. You are trying to find an attorney who understands softball and prefers to keep the case cool. At the same time, you want someone who can slug it out if the other side gets aggressive.

Hardball: If your spouse plays dirty or is being very aggressive, you will want a formidable and aggressive attorney with lots of experience to protect you and slug it out. If you want an especially aggressive attorney, perhaps even a pugilist, be very cautious: you may end up with a tiger by the tail. An acquisitive, mercenary attorney can turn on you as easily as on your spouse.

Avoid situations where you don't like the way the attorney or the staff treat you. Avoid lawyers with a pushy, domineering personality; they may not listen to you or be willing to do things your way. Make sure the attorney knows it is your life and your case; that you are in charge.

Fees and retainer agreements

Divorce actions are always unpredictable, so lawyers rarely quote a flat fee for doing a divorce, but usually charge an hourly rate instead. Call around to see what the going rates are in your area. If, however, you are requesting a specific service, like writing a marital settlement agreement when the terms are all settled, then a flat fee is just what you want. Flat fees have the advantage of being more definite; you know exactly what the service will cost.

You should insist on a *written* retainer agreement in any case that is likely to run over $1,000. The agreement should specify what work is to be done and the fee to be charged or the manner in which the fee will be calculated.

If you have little or no income or other assets, and your spouse has plenty of stable income, savings or other assets, then you should be looking for an attorney who will agree to take your case for out-of-pocket costs and collect all attorney's fees from your spouse. You want the retainer agreement to state clearly that the attorney will *only* seek compensation from your spouse and not from you under any circumstance. Many attorneys will work on this basis, but many won't, so you will have to shop around until you find someone with a good attitude.

If you can, avoid putting up security for your attorney's fees—don't sign a mortgage or trust deed on your home or any other property. It makes it very complicated to change if you become dissatisfied with the service. If this is what the attorney wants, look around for another attorney.

Be very cautious of any attorney who asks for a fee that is contingent on the size of your recovery. That practice is generally inappropriate in divorce cases.

A retainer contract is something you negotiate like any other deal and there is no law that says it has to be a take-it-or-leave-it proposition. Attorneys with that attitude may be arrogant, stubborn and hard to work with on other levels, so keep looking. There are many ways that billing practices can work to your disadvantage, so you will want to examine and give careful thought to the details of any retainer agreement you are asked to sign. Take it home, study it, make sure you understand everything in it before you sign. Pay special attention to things it does not say. Discuss terms you don't understand and terms that you want removed, changed or added. It is okay to request and discuss terms that you would like but don't expect to get. That is the nature of negotiation.

Here is a list of terms to think about and negotiate over, more or less in order of importance to you:
- Be very clear that you do not pay for time spent negotiating the attorney's contract. The attorney is working for himself during that time, so billing should start only after the contract is signed.
- Make sure the retainer paid will be applied to future billings and not kept as a base fee for taking the case. Specify that any unused portions will be returned.
- Define time units billed and how fractions of hours are rounded off; avoid the common practice where you can get billed a quarter hour for a five–minute phone call.

• Request (insist on?) a detailed itemization on each billing that shows the date and time for each task, total time spent, and amount billed.

• Request a monthly billing.

• Inquire about charges, if any, for secretary and staff time. Request that amounts for time billed to secretaries, research assistants, paralegals or associate attorneys be billed separately. This is so you can see exactly what is going on and who is doing it.

• You may want it stated that you will not be responsible for associate attorneys or experts retained without your written consent.

• If your case is not terribly complex, ask that the contract specify that you will not be billed for research time. The high hourly rate implies that the attorney already knows his business.

• Try to get an agreement that you will not be billed for court time spent on continuances that you do not request or for any court time not actually in trial. You really don't want to pay $150 an hour for time spent just sitting around waiting to continue your case to some other day.

Here's a novel idea: consider offering an incentive fee where the attorney gets paid at a higher rate if your case is settled very quickly, in less than some specified number of hours. This rewards the attorney for fast, effective work. Conversely, the rate would go down if your case goes over so many hours or if it goes to trial. This is not a common practice but it may suit your case. It's just one more thing you can negotiate when getting into a retainer agreement.

How to use your lawyer

Using a lawyer efficiently. The most important thing is to be very well prepared whenever you contact a lawyer. Know your facts, know what you want to ask about, and know exactly what you want the lawyer to explain or do for you. Plan each conversation; make an agenda; write down the things you want to talk about; take notes on the content of every conversation; keep track of time spent on all phone calls and meetings. Keep a file for all your notes and all letters and documents. Do as much as possible on the phone and by mail to keep office time at a minimum.

Regard your attorney as a resource, not someone you cling to or depend on for emotional support and stability. A lawyer is not the right person to make your decisions or lead your life—you are. Lawyers cost too much for you to use them for sympathy and consolation—that's what family, friends and counselors are for.

When you talk to a lawyer, stick to the facts and don't just chat, ramble, or complain about things your spouse did unless you actually want your lawyer to do something about it. Don't take your anger to an attorney; you want your best interests represented, not your emotions.

Taking control of your own case. Being in control of your own case and your own life is the single best thing you can do in any divorce, so it is essential that you have a lawyer who can work cheerfully on that basis. If you are well prepared and business like, that will help the lawyer to see that you are in charge of things, but you should actually *say* that's how you want it to be. Tell the lawyer that you want good advice and will rely on the lawyer's experience, but that you expect to make decisions that concern the tone and strategy of the case. Ask that you be sent copies of all documents and letters. Let the attorney know that you expect phone calls to be answered by the next working day. These little things let the lawyer know you are the boss. After all, you pay the bills.

Using a lawyer for specific tasks. Instead of hiring a lawyer to get you a divorce, it may be far more cost-effective to use the lawyer just for information or advice on specific subjects. That may be all the legal help you will need. If not, you can always go back for more help later. After you have organized all your facts and read about how the law works in your case, if you still have questions about the law or what the likely outcome will be in your county, write all your questions down and ask a lawyer.

You may decide to have a lawyer help with your marital settlement agreement, either to draft one or just to check over one you have made yourself. If you get stuck or confused at any point in your divorce, that's a good time to go for help. The more specific and prepared you can be, the more you will get for your money.

How to fire your lawyer

You have a right to discharge your attorney at any time for any reason or no reason at all, whether or not any money is owed. Of course, you will continue to owe your former lawyer for time spent working on your case.

If your lawyer is not performing to your satisfaction, you may want to send a letter (keep copies) setting out very specifically what needs to be changed. If there is no improvement, start shopping for another lawyer. Some things can't be changed: for example, if you lose trust and confidence in your lawyer, get another one or take over the case yourself. Nothing is worse than feeling trapped in a bad relationship with your own attorney.

If your spouse has an attorney, it would be unwise to fire your old attorney until you have another, and your new attorney will arrange the transfer. However, if your spouse has no attorney, you can consider taking over the case yourself.

If you discharge your attorney to take over yourself, do it in writing *and keep a copy of the letter*. If the attorney has filed documents in court, you must also file a Discharge of Attorney naming yourself as the new attorney "In Pro Per" or "Pro Se," which means that you represent yourself. There is a form on the next page that you can copy and use. Fill it out, sign it, and make three copies. Have someone (not you) mail a copy to your ex-attorney, your spouse and your spouse's attorney, if any. That person signs the Proof of Service at the bottom, then you file it with the court clerk. Send a letter to your ex-attorney politely explaining that you have taken over your own case and request that all files and papers be immediately forwarded to you.

An attorney cannot ethically delay turning over files and documents merely to pressure you into payment of amounts owed. Failure to promptly forward files as you request is a breach of the attorney's ethical duty to you. In case of unreasonable delay, fire off a letter of complaint to the local and State Bar associations with copies to your old attorney. Meanwhile, you can always get copies of court documents from the court clerk.

```
 1 │ Name:
   │ Address:
 2 │ City, State, Zip:
   │ Phone:
 3 │ Declarant, In Pro Per / Pro Se

 4 │

 5 │                         (type in title of court)

 6 │

 7 │

 8 │ In re the marriage of:          )
   │                                 )   Case No.
 9 │ Petitioner/Plaintiff:           )
   │                                 )   DISCHARGE OF ATTORNEY
10 │   and                           )
   │                                 )
11 │ Respondent/Defendant:           )
   │                                 )
12 │ _____  )

13 │ I, _____ , as the

14 │ Petitioner/Plaintiff/Respondent/Defendant in the within action, hereby
   │ discharge my attorney _____
15 │ whose business address is _____ . All
   │ further notices, pleadings and other communications of any kind in this
16 │ case should be directed to me as follows:

17 │                         Name:
   │                      Address:
18 │              City, State, Zip:

19 │ Dated: _____      _____
```

DECLARANT

PROOF OF SERVICE

I, _____ , declare that: I am over the age of eighteen years and not a party to the cause; I am employed in, or am a resident of, _____ , where the mailing occured. I further declare that I am familiar with the practice for collection and processing of mail with the United States Postal Service. This same day in the ordinary course of business, I caused to be served the following document(s):

Discharge of Attorney

by placing a copy of each document in a separate envelope addressed to each addressee, respectively, as follows:

Name of party: Name of attorney:
Address: Address:
City, State, Zip: City, State, Zip:

I then sealed each envelope and, with the postage thereon fully prepaid, I placed each for deposit in the United States Postal Service this same day, following ordinary business practices.
I declare under penalty of perjury that the foregoing is true and correct.

Executed on: _____   Signed: _____

APPENDIX A
Sample marital settlement agreement

A *simple* marital settlement agreement (MSA) is included here to show you what one looks like and for you to use as a guide in thinking about your own MSA.

Caution!

• This is a generic agreement. Many states or courts have specific requirements that must be included in MSAs. This one would not, for example, be acceptable in California. If you try to draft your own, look for a good, recent book or kit for your state with an MSA in it. If you can't find one, and if you can't afford to get professional help, use this one and see what happens. Do your best with what you've got.

• This agreement is mostly suitable for simple cases—a few household goods, autos, a few debts ....nothing too big or complicated.

• If you go much beyond this sample MSA, it should be drafted by a family law specialist. Do **not** let a paralegal draft your MSA unless you have a very simple, low value case and the paralegal copies an MSA from a good book specifically for your state. Do not use Uncle Joe's MSA or anyone else's as a guide; it may be from a different state or a different time, and it will certainly be for different people. Get one professionally tailored to your needs and today's laws.

• **The three before's:** If you get help, be sure to get your information and advice *before* you state your position to your spouse, *before* you draft your MSA, and *before* you sign anything. *After* is usually too late.

Subjects not covered: Some subjects are too complex or tricky to be covered here; all the clever clauses lawyers use would fill a large book. Below is a list of common situations that require professional advice and drafting. If you have any of these in your case, get help.

• Family support (instead of child support, to get tax savings);

• Zero child support in joint custody cases;

• Security for payment of debts or amounts to be paid later;

• Spousal support—stepping up or down, amount and duration depending on various conditions, termination in cases where there is a long marriage;

• Sale of a major asset to take place after MSA signed—protection of respective interests until sale and allocation of costs;

• Tax consequences on sale of a major item—maximizing tax savings, minimizing tax liability;

- Equalization payments;
- Future interest in a pension plan, to be distributed upon reaching retirement age;
- Self-employment, solely owned business, side-line business—valuation and division;
- Intellectual property—ownership and future value of music, writings, paintings, software, inventions, etc.

Technicalities:

Secure promises to pay: A debt between spouses to settle their divorce case can be discharged in bankruptcy; so can promises to hold a spouse harmless from certain debts or liability. Such promises should be secured whenever possible, preferably by a trust deed (mortgage) on real property.

Modification: Orders for child support or custody can always be modified to accommodate changed circumstances. Spousal support can possibly be modified *unless* your agreement very clearly (and with correct wording) states that it can't; check local laws and rules.

Changes: If you later agree to change your arrangements for custody, visitation or support, be sure to do it in writing and then get your Judgment modified. Informal understandings won't affect your written agreement; written agreements won't change your old Judgment—it remains in effect until it is formally modified.

Reconciliation: A marital settlement agreement is generally not canceled if you reconcile later; verify local laws. To terminate a written agreement, you will have to change or revoke it in writing.

Warning: Think carefully before signing an agreement for less than your fair share of property and support. People sometimes do this, but are usually sorry later. Don't give away valuable rights because you feel guilty, or to make your soon-to-be ex-spouse like you better, or just to get it over with. It is very difficult and extremely expensive to try to break an agreement.

Details: You will need the original and three copies of the agreement. When signing, both spouses should also initial each page at the bottom and initial any alterations or corrections that have been written into the document. **Notarize:** a growing number of courts want notarized signatures on MSAs prepared without an attorney. It is a good idea to notarize, even if you don't have to.

Doing your own MSA: If you decide to write your own marital settlement agreement, use the parts below that apply to you. Change the wording to suit your needs; disregard what doesn't fit. Many courts want documents typed double-spaced. Do it that way, just to be sure. Do not leave out boiler plate paragraphs X to XV. Use clear and specific wording because vague terms with more than one possible meaning cannot be enforced. Your MSA will, in effect, become your Judgment, so it *must* be right. If you have trouble understanding the agreement, or wording it to fit your own case, get help.

MARITAL SETTLEMENT AGREEMENT

I, _____, Husband, and I, _____, Wife, agree as follows:

I. GENERALLY: We are now husband and wife. We were married on the ____ day of _____, 19___, and separated on the ____ day of _____, 19___. We make this agreement with reference to the following facts:

   A. Children: There are (no children/the following minor children of the parties born into this marriage): **list**

Child's name	Birth date	Sex

   B. Unhappy and irreconcilable differences have arisen between us which have caused the irremediable breakdown of our marriage. There is no possible chance for reconciliation.
   C. We now intend, by this agreement, to make a final and complete settlement of all of our rights and obligations concerning child custody, child support, spousal support, and division of property.

II. SEPARATION: We agree to live separately and apart, and, except for the duties and obligations imposed and assumed under this agreement, each shall be free from interference and control of the other as fully as if he or she were single.

III. PARENTING PLAN: **(choose one)**:
   A. Joint custody: Husband and Wife shall jointly share the legal and physical custody and care of our minor children. Our parenting relationship shall be guided by the following parenting plan: (**put down your parenting plan in as much detail as possible, example below**).
   B. Joint legal custody with primary physical custody: Husband and Wife shall jointly share the legal custody of the minor children of the parties, and (Husband/Wife) shall have the primary physical custody of

said children. Our parenting relationship shall be guided by the following plan: **(parenting plan, example below)**.

    C. Sole custody and visitation: (Husband/Wife) shall have the sole legal and physical custody of the minor children of the parties, subject to the right of (Wife/Husband/other) to visit said children as follows: **(put down the parenting plan in as much detail as possible, example below)**.

PARENTING SCHEDULE: **Don't just copy this plan—think about it and change it to fit your case.**

1. Parenting Schedule:
    a. <u>Weekends</u>: Alternate weekends, beginning **(date)** from Friday at 6 p.m. until Sunday at 7 p.m. The weekend shall be extended to 7 p.m. on Monday if the Monday is a holiday when the children are scheduled to be with (Mother/Father).

    b. <u>Spring School Vacation</u>: During the children's spring vacation from school, (Father's/Mother's) parenting time shall be from 6:00 p.m. Friday to 6 p.m. Wednesday if his/her regular weekend is *before* the vacation, or shall be from 6 p.m. on Wednesday to 7:00 p.m. Sunday if his/her regular weekend is *after* the vacation.

    c. <u>Summer School Vacation</u>: Six weeks during the children's school vacation time during the summer with starting and ending times to be agreed upon by the parties. During these six weeks, the children will spend alternate weekends with (Mother/Father) from Friday at 6 p.m. until Sunday at 7 p.m. The weekend shall be extended to 7 p.m. on Monday if the Monday is a holiday when the children are scheduled to be with (him/her).

    d. <u>Holiday Schedule</u>:
<u>Thanksgiving</u>:
In odd-numbered years, from 6 p.m. on the Wednesday before Thanksgiving until 6 p.m. on the following Sunday.
    <u>Christmas:</u>
In odd-numbered years, from noon on December 26 until 6 p.m. on the day before school resumes in January.
In even-numbered years, from 6 p.m. on the last school day before the Christmas school vacation until noon on December 26.
    or—
Seven consecutive days, including any regularly scheduled weekend time, during the children's Christmas holiday from school. The starting and ending times shall be agreed upon by the parties.
    <u>Other Holidays</u>: As agreed by the parties.

3. Each parent shall be responsible for picking up the children at the beginning of his or her parenting time.

4. Either parent may designate any competent adult to pick up the children and to be with the children when they are picked up.

5. Each parent shall give at least 24 hours advance notice to the other parent if he or she must change the schedule. The parent requesting the change shall be responsible for any additional child care costs that result from the change.

6. Both parents will cooperate in finding alternate child care for those periods when regular child care is not available, and the cost of said child care shall be included when the parties establish how the cost of child care is to be shared.

7. Neither parent may remove, or cause to be removed, the minor children from the state of _____ without 30 days prior written notice to the other parent. This provision applies to vacations *and trips* outside of the state of California

8. Neither parent may change his or her residence or the residence of the minor children without 60 days prior written notice to the other parent.

Options: consider other provisions such as a) visits with grandparents; b) a successor to visitation rights in case of death of visiting parent; c) written notice to other spouse in case of changes in health, education, well-being, educational progress; d) agree to provide documents to allow spouse to inquire directly with doctors, hospitals, school personnel.
More options: That the children will keep the father's surname and not take on the mother's maiden name or name of any new spouse, at least until the child is old enough to make that decision. Some spouses want an agreement about the children's religious upbringing and education.

IV. SUPPORT OF CHILDREN: We agree that this agreement is in the best interest of the children and that the needs of the children will be adequately met by the agreed amount.
As and for child support,_____shall pay to _____
$ _____ per month per child, a total of $ _____ per month, payable on the ____day of each month, beginning on the ___day of _____, 19__. Support shall continue for each child until said child dies, marries, becomes self-supporting, or reaches majority, whichever occurs first. When any child becomes ineligible to receive support or circumstances otherwise change, the parties will stipulate to. or apply to the court for, a new support order.

As additional child support, (Husband / Wife) shall obtain and maintain in force a policy of insurance providing major medical, dental and vision coverage for each child for the duration of the support obligation. The child's health costs that are not covered by any policy of health insurance shall be paid for by (Husband/Wife/shared in some percentage).

Life insurance option: In addition, during the term of the support obligation for each child, (Husband / Wife / both equally/ other percentage sharing) shall carry and maintain a policy of life insurance in the amount of

$_____$, and shall name as sole irrevocable beneficiaries (Wife / Husband / said minor children), and shall not borrow, assign or otherwise encumber said policy.

VI. SUPPORT PAYMENTS TO SPOUSE: The parties agree that the following amount of spousal support (does/does not) completely meet the current needs of the recipient for support. **(Use A or B)**

A. Waiver of Right to Support: In consideration of the other terms of this agreement, and whereas both spouses are fully self-supporting, **(Choose one of the following):**

...there will be no order for spousal support at this time, but the court shall retain jurisdiction over spousal support.

...both parties waive all right or claim which they may now have to receive support or maintenance from the other. No court shall have jurisdiction to award spousal support at any time regardless of any circumstances that may arise.

B. In consideration of the other terms of this marital settlement agreement, $_____$ agrees to pay to $_____$ the sum of $\$_____$ per month, payable on the $\_\_\_$ day of each month, beginning $_____$, 19$\_\_$, and continuing until **(any or all of the following— some certain date, the death of the payer, death of the recipient, remarriage of the recipient, cohabitation, some other *precise* condition)** whichever occurs first.

Optional: ...Said (termination date/amount) is absolute and no court shall have jurisdiction to modify the (amount/ duration/ amount or duration) of spousal support at any time regardless of any circumstances that may arise.

VII. CONFIRMATION OF SEPARATE PROPERTY:

A. The following property was and is the separate property of Wife, and Husband confirms it to her and waives any claim to or interest in it: **list—describe clearly; for example, use auto license numbers, assessor's parcel numbers and legal description for real estate.**

B. The following property was and is the separate property of Husband, and Wife confirms it to him and waives any claim to or interest in it: **list—describe clearly.**

VIII. DIVISION OF MARITAL PROPERTY AND DEBTS: The parties warrant and declare under penalty of perjury that the assets and liabilities divided in this agreement constitute all their marital assets and liabilities. In the event that the division is unequal, the parties knowingly and intelligently waive an equal division of the marital property.

A. Husband is awarded and assigned the following assets as his share of the marital property: **(list each item or groups of items. Give legal description of real estate including assessor's parcel number and license number for vehicles).**

B. Wife is awarded and assigned the following assets as her share of the marital property: **(list).**

Alternate for cases with little or no significant property or bills: Husband and Wife agree that their marital property and bills are minimal, and that they have already divided everything to their mutual satisfaction. Each

Sample marital settlement agreement

hereby transfers and quitclaims to the other any and all interest in any property in the possession of the other, and agrees that whatever property the other may possess is now the sole and separate property of the other.

C. Husband shall pay the following debts promptly when due, and indemnify and hold Wife harmless therefrom: **(list—identify clearly, give value of each item).**

D. Wife shall pay the following debts promptly when due, and indemnify and hold Husband harmless therefrom: **(list—as above).**

E. Husband and Wife each promise the other that they shall not incur any debt or obligation for which the other may be liable, and each agrees that if any claim be brought seeking to hold one liable for the subsequent debts of the other, or for any act or omission of the other, then each will hold the other harmless, and defend such claim.

F. If either party decides to claim any rights under bankruptcy laws, that party must notify the other of this intention in writing at least fourteen days before filing the petition, including the name, address and phone number of the attorney, if any, who represents the party in that petition and the court in which the petition will be filed. The party receiving notice will have five business days to elect to participate jointly with the notifying party in a consolidation proceeding and may choose to be represented by the same attorney, if any.

Note about pension plans: If there is a marital interest in a pension plan, it must be dealt with in your MSA. If it is to be given entirely to the employee-spouse, list it in item A or B above. If the pension will be paid to both spouses in the future, you can't do the MSA or the Judgment orders yourself. Get help.

Note about family home: spouses may agree to a) sell and divide the home now; or b) a buy-out by one spouse, possibly with a promissory note to the other (payments may be deferred to some future time or event); or c) joint ownership of family residence, as follows:

G. FAMILY HOME: Title to the family residence located at (address, assessor's parcel number) shall be placed in the names of Husband and Wife as tenants in common, each holding a 50% undivided interest therein (or some other percentages). The Wife and the minor children may continue to occupy the property until 1) the support obligation for all children has terminated, or 2) Wife dies or remarries, or 3) Wife no longer has custody of any child of the parties, or 4) Wife and children cease to reside in the home, or 5) Wife becomes 60 days delinquent in any payment set forth in this paragraph, or 6) (...some other date or condition). On termination of Wife's right to occupy the house, it shall be sold and the proceeds, after deducting costs of the sale, shall be distributed according to their percentage of ownership. Wife shall make all payments on existing encumbrances, together with taxes, insurance and other assessments, without right to reimbursement, such payments being considered fair value for occupancy. Capital expenditures for improvements may be made when agreed by the parties, and the cost divided equally between them. Individual outlays for $500 or less shall be deemed maintenance. **Taxes from sale of property: You should indicate how taxes that arise from the sale of the home will be shared—all to one spouse, each spouse to bear his or her own tax liability, or spouses to share any tax liabilities from the sale of the home.**

IX. TAXES:

A. Any tax refunds for the current fiscal year shall be distributed as follows: **(specify).**

B. Any tax deficiencies for the current year shall be paid as follows: **(specify)**.

C. For any year in which support payments for said child are not over ___ days in arrears, the parent paying support may claim the tax exemption for **(names of children)** and the recipient will execute a waiver of the right to claim the exemption for that year.

X. RESERVATION OF JURISDICTION: The parties agree that the court shall have jurisdiction to make whatever orders may be necessary or desirable to carry out this agreement and to divide equally between the parties any marital assets or liabilities omitted from division under this agreement.

XI. ADVICE OF COUNSEL: The parties recognize that the termination of the marriage, issues of child custody, visitation, child and spousal support, and division of marital property will be determined by this instrument. We recognize that we each have a right to seek advice from independent counsel of our own choosing and that we knowingly and with due regard for the importance of same have elected to proceed with this agreement.

XII. EXECUTION OF INSTRUMENTS: Each agrees to execute and deliver any documents, make all endorsements, and do all acts which are necessary or convenient to carry out the terms of this agreement.

XIII. PRESENTATION TO COURT:
This agreement shall be presented to the court in any divorce proceeding between the parties, it shall be incorporated into the Judgment therein, the parties shall be ordered to comply with all its provisions, and all warranties and remedies provided in this agreement shall be preserved.

XIV. DISCLOSURES: Each party has made a full and honest disclosure to the other of all current finances and assets, and each enters into this agreement in reliance thereon. Each warrants to the other and declares under penalty of perjury that the assets and liabilities divided in this agreement constitute all of their marital assets and liabilities.

XV. BINDING EFFECT: This agreement, and each provision thereof, is expressly made binding upon heirs, assigns, executors, administrators, representatives, and successors in interest of each party.

Dated: _____ _____Husband

Dated: _____ _____ Wife

Sample marital settlement agreement

APPENDIX B
Recommended Reading

There are a lot of very good books out there, but to save you the trouble of wading through shelves of titles, we asked some leading counselors which books they regarded as classics. Asterisks indicate the author's pick. This isn't the definitive list, just a place to start, so keep looking, keep reading, keep learning. Ask people you know what helped them; that's the best way.

For Everyone:
Crazy Times, Abigail Trafford. Harper & Row.
* Dance of Anger, Harriet Goldhor Lerner. Harper & Row, 1985.
* Getting to Yes: Negotiating Agreement Without Giving In, Fisher & Ury. Penguin.
Love is Letting Go of Fear, Gerald G. Jampolsky. Celestial Arts, 1979.
* How to Survive the Loss of a Love, Colgrove, Bloomfield & McWilliams. Bantam.
The Divorce Book, McKay, Rogers, Blades, & Gosse. New Harbinger, 1984.
Uncoupling: the Art of Coming Apart, Mannes & Sheresky. Viking, 1982.

For Parents:
Helping Your Child Succeed After Divorce, Florence Bienenfeld. Hunter House, 1987.
Helping Your Children With Divorce, Edward Teyber, Ph.D.
* Parent's Book About Divorce, Richard A. Gardner. Doubleday, 1977.

* Surviving the Breakup, Wallerstein and Kelly. Basic Books, 1980.
What Every Child Would Like Parents to Know About Divorce, Lee Salk. Warner Books, 1978.

Shared Custody:
* Mom's House, Dad's House, Isolina Ricci. McMillan, 1980.
Sharing Parenthood After Divorce, Ciji Ware. Viking, 1982.

For Fathers:
101 Ways to Be a Long Distance Super-Dad, George Newman. Blossom Valley Press, 1981.
The Father's Role, Ed. by Michael E. Lamb. Wylie & Sons, 1986.

For Scholars:
* The Process of Divorce, Kenneth Kressel. Basic Books, 1985.